FACTS AT YOUR FINGERTIPS

WORLD WAR II

FACTS AT YOUR FINGERTIPS

WORLD WAR II

BROWN
BEAR
BOOKS

Published by Brown Bear Books

An imprint of
The Brown Reference Group Ltd
68 Topstone Road
Redding
Connecticut
06896
USA

www.brownreference.com

Library of Congress Cataloging-in-Publication Data
available upon request.

ISBN-13 978-1-933834-50-4

Author: Antony Shaw
Editorial Director: Lindsey Lowe
Senior Managing Editor: Tim Cooke
Designer: Sarah Williams
Editor: Peter Darman

Printed in the United States of America

CONTENTS

To those who lived through it, World War I (1914–1918) was "the War to End All Wars." Its upheaval and sacrifice were necessary to establish a new, stable and peaceful world order. In fact, the end of World War I created many of the conditions that would lead directly to the outbreak of an even more destructive conflict: World War II.

By 1918, Germany was in dire straits: its population was near to starvation, its army and navy in disarray. The Treaty of Versailles of June 1919 removed Germany's overseas possessions and authorized the Allied occupation of the Rhineland. The treaty blamed Germany for starting the war and imposed huge fines, or reparations, for the damage inflicted by Germany during World War I.

The Germans struggled to pay. Their economy was almost bankrupt even before the world economy slumped in 1921. In 1922, Germany defaulted on reparations payments for the second year running. In retaliation, France occupied the Ruhr, the center of German industry. The move reduced the already slim chances of Germany paying any reparations, and increased hostility between the two countries.

The removal of the Ruhr's industrial contribution to the German economy had a calamitous impact on the German currency, which plummeted in value. Overnight, savings were wiped out, leaving millions penniless and destitute, their careers, hopes, and finances destroyed.

The rise of Adolf Hitler

In such an atmosphere, people searched desperately for answers. Many Germans found them in the vitriolic oratory of an ex-soldier named Adolf Hitler, who belonged to the Nationalsozialistische Deutsche Arbeiterpartei (National Socialist German Workers' Party, or "Nazi" Party). Hitler argued that the failure of the Weimar government to cope with war debts and inflation made a radical alternative necessary.

Despite the failure of Hitler's attempted coup in 1923 in Munich, Nazi Party membership grew throughout the 1920s. The worldwide Great Depression that began in 1929 played into the Nazis' hands. Germans were enthusiastic to hear Hitler blame the economic crisis on what he termed "unpatriotic" Jews

Adolf Hitler became Chancellor of Germany in 1933 and soon established a dictatorship. He was obsessed with the creation of German "living space" in Eastern Europe.

and communist conspiracies. In 1932 elections, Hitler polled 36.9 percent of the vote. After he ingratiated himself with German president Paul von Hindenburg, the latter invited Hitler to become chancellor in 1933. Once in power, Hitler established a dictatorship and then took radical steps he felt would revitalize the economy, including the abolition of trade unions and the persecution of Jewish businesses. He also renounced the Treaty of Versailles, began to rearm Germany, and sent troops to reoccupy the Rhineland.

Expanding the Reich

Hitler now looked for *Lebensraum* ("living space") beyond Germany. As Austria and Czechoslovakia were absorbed into the Third Reich, the Western democracies hesitated. Many people in both Britain and France believed that the terms imposed on Germany by the Treaty of Versailles had been harsh, and that appeasing Hitler (assenting to his demands) would lay a basis for a lasting peace. They were mistaken. The hope that the Munich Agreement of September 1938, whereby the Sudetenland was ceded to Germany, would lead to "peace in our time" was also wrong. In March 1939, Germany occupied the rest of Czechoslovakia.

Mussolini's Italy

Hitler's belligerence was matched by his allies in Europe and Asia. In Italy, for example, Benito Mussolini's fascist regime had achieved some notable results, such as the establishment of a relatively stable economy. Mussolini had also built up Italy's army, navy, and air force with a view to military conquests. Realizing that his armed forces still lacked the most modern equipment, however, he picked his military opponents carefully. His attack on Ethiopia (then Abyssinia) in Africa was regarded with disgust by other European nations, as Italian warplanes dropped bombs and poison gas on people who fought only with spears. However, the war confirmed the impotence of the League of Nations, the body set up after World War I to resolve international disputes. The league failed to rally any of its members to take effective action against Italy.

The Axis Alliance

Meanwhile, in East Asia, Japan had also begun to flex its muscles. Having defeated Russia in the war of 1904–1905, Japan's military commanders had gained huge influence in the affairs of their country. In 1910, Japan annexed Korea, and, in 1931, Japan went on to

Italian tanks in the Spanish Civil War (1936–1939), in which some of Mussolini's forces gained valuable combat experience.

overrun Manchuria in northern China. When the League of Nations protested, Japan simply resigned from the organization. Later, in 1936, Japan signed the anticommunist Anti-Comintern Pact with Germany and Italy to create a Rome–Berlin–Tokyo Axis. The Axis was seemingly further strengthened when Hitler and Joseph Stalin, the Soviet leader, signed a nonaggression pact on August 23, 1939, in which a secret clause divided up Poland between them in any future war.

Poland now became the focus of Hitler's attention. Re-created after World War I, it had been given access to the sea via a corridor of land that reached the Baltic at Danzig. The land had been German territory, and Hitler was determined it would be so again. Danzig was, in theory, a "free city" run by the League of Nations, but in reality the Nazis had gained control of the city in 1934. Hitler argued that it and the strip of land that divided Germany and East Prussia should be returned to the Reich. Few people in the West knew or cared about this Polish Corridor, but in March 1939 Britain and France took the fateful step of pledging themselves to the defense of Poland, which neither of them was in a military position to do. When German armies entered Poland on September 1, 1939, Britain and France had no choice but to declare war on Germany. This they did, two days later. World War II had begun, little more than two decades after the end of the first great conflict.

As **1939 began,** three years of mounting international tension encompassing the Spanish Civil War, the Anschluss (union) of Germany and Austria, Hitler's occupation of the Sudetenland, and the German invasion of Czechoslovakia had left Europe on the brink of war. Modern critics often wonder why France and Britain did not make a stronger stand against Adolf Hitler in the 1930s, and, by doing so, perhaps have prevented the world being again plunged into global conflict so soon after World War I had almost wiped out an entire generation.

But both had their reasons for caution. France shared a border with Germany, had a smaller population and economy, and would not have been able to defeat Hitler's reinvigorated military machine on its own. Britain faced a different set of problems. Its empire in East Asia was threatened by Japan's increasingly militaristic stance, and provoking war in Europe could have seen a disastrous division of British armed forces. However, a deeper reason for both Britain and France to "appease" Hitler—give in to some of his demands—was that both countries had been deeply traumatized by the carnage of World War I and were desperate to avoid another costly European conflict.

Austria and Czechoslovakia

So it was that in 1938, Britain and France did little to prevent Adolf Hitler from declaring on March 13 that Austria—Hitler's nation of birth—would henceforth become a province of the German Reich.

The next month, Hitler's territorial ambitions again gave cause for alarm, when the dictator began to demand that the German population living in the Sudetenland region of Czechoslovakia should be brought back into the German empire, or "Reich." This time, in a bid to head off a military confrontation, British Prime Minister Neville Chamberlain called a conference at Munich on September 30, 1938. It was attended by Britain, France, Italy, and Germany, and the outcome was that the Czechs were told to evacuate

A German Heinkel He III warplane attacks Warsaw during Germany's invasion of Poland in 1939. Aircraft were a vital component of Hitler's "Blitzkrieg" combat strategy, acting as mobile artillery and clearing the way for fast-moving ground assault units.

the Sudetenland by October 10. If they did not, they would get no assistance in resisting German aggression. Chamberlain triumphantly claimed that the Munich Agreement delivered "peace in our time." However, within a year, Europe was at war.

The road to war

On March 15, 1939, following unrest in the region, Hitler sent his military forces in to occupy the whole of Czechoslovakia. On April 7, 1939, Hitler's ally Italian dictator Benito Mussolini, eager for military conquests of his own, sent Italian forces into Albania and easily achieved victory there.

Against this backdrop, Hitler now looked toward Poland and restated his claims to the city of Danzig and the strip of land known as the Polish Corridor. Having secured a nonaggression pact with the Soviet Union's leader, Joseph Stalin, Hitler felt that any German incursion into Poland would not be opposed by Britain or France, and so, on September 1, 1939, having fabricated a Polish raid into German territory to use as an excuse, Hitler's Nazi forces rolled across the border into Poland, easily overrunning the country in short order. To Hitler's surprise, Britain and France opposed him, declaring war on Germany on September 3, 1939. World War II had begun.

The phoney war

For the next few months, Western Europe was quiet during what became known as "the phoney war". Preparations for war continued in earnest in both France and Britain, but there were few signs of conflict. Civilians who had been evacuated from London in the first few months gradually drifted back into Britain's capital city. Meanwhile, gas masks were distributed, air raid shelters were constructed, and everyone waited uneasily for the war proper to begin.

In eastern Europe and Scandinavia, however, there was nothing phoney about the war. With the Ribbentrop Pact signed between the Soviet Union and Germany in August, in September the USSR followed Germany into Poland, which was carved up between the two invaders by the end of the year. Russia then continued its aggression by going on to invade Finland.

INVASION OF POLAND

BATTLE OF THE ATLANTIC

A German force of 53 divisions, supported by 2,085 aircraft, invaded Poland on September 1, 1939. Poland's armed forces were quickly defeated. On September 17, in accordance with the Soviet secret pact with Germany, the Red Army also invaded. By early October, Poland had been overrun and the campaign was over.

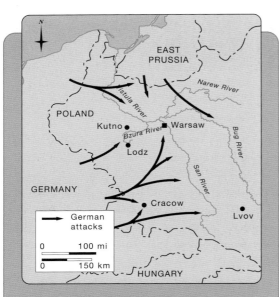

INVASION OF POLAND

Location Poland

Date September 1–October 6, 1939

Commanders and forces German: Army Group North (Third and Fourth Armies, Colonel-General Fedor von Bock); Army Group South (Eighth, Tenth, and Fourteenth Armies, Colonel-General Gerd von Rundstedt); Polish: Modlin Army (General Emil Krukowicz-Przedrzymirski), Narew Special Operational Group (General Czeslaw Mlot-Fijalkowski), Pomorze Army (General Wladyslaw Bortnowski), Poznan Army (General Tadeusz Kutrzeba), Lodz Army (General Juliusz Rommel), Cracow Army (General Antoni Szylling), Carpathian Army (General Kazimierz Fabrycy), Prusy Army (High Command)

Force levels German: 1,250,000 troops, 2,511 tanks, 5,805 artillery pieces, and 4,019 antitank guns; Polish: 1,000,000 troops, 2,800 artillery pieces, 500 tanks

Aircraft German: 2,085; Polish: 360

Casualties German: 10,500 killed; Polish: 50,000 killed, 750,000 taken prisoner

Key actions The Battle of the Bzura, September 11–20, 1939, saw the the German Eighth and Tenth Armies trap and then destroy the Polish Poznan Army, which amounted to around 25 percent of the entire Polish field force.

Key effects In the swift defeat of Polish forces in 1939, Germany had won the first of what would become a series of devastating Blitzkrieg attacks—from the Low Countries and France to the Soviet Union—that shattered the military balance of power in Europe between 1939 and 1941. However, following his successful invasion of Poland, Adolf Hitler now faced Britain and France's declarations of war.

The Battle of the Atlantic was a fight for Britain's very survival. If Germany had prevented merchant ships from carrying food, raw materials, troops, and equipment (including tanks and other military vehicles) from North America to Britain, the outcome of World War II could have been very different. It is distinctly possible that Britain may have been forced to surrender to Hitler.

After June 1940, the German conquest of Norway and France gave the Nazis forward bases, which they used to increase the range of their U-boats (submarines) and also allowed long-range aircraft to patrol over the Atlantic, carrying out reconnaissance for the U-boats and attacking Allied shipping. The British were forced to divert their own shipping away from vulnerable home ports, and were faced with the need to provide convoys with naval escorts for greater stretches of the journey from North America.

The crisis point came in May 1943. Admiral Dönitz, head of the German Navy, now had 200 operational U-boats, and it became a matter of whether the Allies could build merchant ships fast enough to replace those being sunk. The mass production of "Liberty Ships" in U.S. shipyards, however, helped to ensure that the Allies would win this race. At sea, new tactics and technology, including an improved "Ultra" intelligence-gathering operation, helped the Allies to turn the tide of the battle. This was not the end of the German threat in the Atlantic, but thereafter it was greatly diminished.

BATTLE OF THE ATLANTIC

Location Atlantic Ocean

Date September 1939–May 1943

Commanders and forces German: 1,000 U-boats (Rear-Admiral Karl Dönitz); British: 9 battleships, 4 aircraft carriers, 35 cruisers, 95 destroyers, 25 submarines (Admiral Sir Charles Forbes)

Casualties German: 19,000 killed (U-boat crews); Allied: 85,000 killed

Key actions After taking heavy losses in the first part of the war, from early 1943 onward British strategy and equipment improved. More aggressive antisubmarine tactics, better depth charges, and the fitting of long-range aircraft with improved radar ensured that U-boat losses rose. A total of 45 German submarines were destroyed in April and May 1943. Dönitz, seeing that such losses could not be tolerated, called off the battle on May 23, 1943. Although the German U-boat threat did not completely disappear, after this time it was greatly diminished.

Key effects The U-boat threat was probably the single most serious threat to Britain during the war. If the Germans had been able to deploy more U-boats in 1940 and 1941, the course of World War II would have been very different, with Britain perhaps starved into submission.

WINTER WAR

A Soviet force of 600,000 men, backed by air and naval power, attacked Finland on November 30, 1939. As aircraft bombed Helsinki, Field Marshal Karl von Mannerheim led the Finnish defense with a mainly reservist force, inferior in numbers and arms. However, he managed to block the main Soviet thrust through the Karelian Isthmus by reinforcing the Mannerheim Line fortifications, which ran through rugged terrain and forest.

Other Soviet forces attacked eastern and northern Finland and also launched failed amphibious assaults on the south coast. As the campaign progressed, Finnish troops exploited their familiarity with the terrain and their ability to ski through snow-covered areas to launch raids on Red Army units bogged down by the weather.

On January 7, 1940, General Semyon Timoshenko assumed command of the Soviet invasion forces. After reorganizing and reequipping, his forces began an attack on the Mannerheim Line on January 12. The Finns completed a withdrawal to a secondary zone of defense by February 17. Secret peace negotiations had begun in January and the war ended on March 13, but the Finnish Army had not capitulated. Finland remained independent, but had to surrender the Karelian Isthmus and Hangö—around 10 percent of its territory.

WINTER WAR

Location Finland

Date November 30, 1939–March 13, 1940

Commanders and forces Finnish: Isthmus Army (Lieutenant General H. Österman), IV Corps (Major General J. Hägglund), Reserve (Major General V. Tuompo). Total: 337,000; Soviet: Seventh Army (General V. F. Jakolev), Eighth Army (General I. N. Habarov), Ninth Army (General M. P. Duhanov), Fourteenth Army (General V. A. Frolov). Total: 600,000

Casualties Finnish: 25,000 killed and 45,500 wounded: Soviet: 126,875 killed and 391,783 wounded

Key actions On February 1, 1940, the Red Army began its offensive in Karelia. Some 600,000 men were committed to the attack. The Finns had six divisions in the front line and three in reserve. Finnish positions were pounded by 300,000 artillery shells on the first day, with Soviet artillery mustering 440 guns in the Summa sector alone. The Soviets also deployed close air support all along the front. The Red Army attacked for three days non-stop, paused for a day, then resumed the offensive for a further three days. Finnish forces were gradually worn down by the onslaught.

Key effects The Red Army learned some valuable lessons from the Winter War: infantry tactics needed to be flexible; there needed to be greater coordination between different units; battle training should be realistic; and winter clothing was imperative for winter warfare. Absorbing these lessons, the Red Army would become a more effective force in the run-up to Operation Barbarossa in June 1941.

BATTLE OF THE RIVER PLATE

The German pocket battleship Admiral Graf Spee *is scuttled after being trapped in the waters off neutral Uruguay.*

After sinking several Allied merchant ships in the Atlantic, the German pocket battleship *Admiral Graf Spee* was sighted on December 13, 1939, off the Río de la Plata estuary by a British naval group consisting of the cruisers *Exeter*, *Ajax,* and *Achilles*, commanded by Commodore H. Harwood. At 06:14 hours, Harwood's ships attacked, but the *Graf Spee* damaged *Exeter* and then made for neutral Montevideo, Uruguay, where its commander, Captain Hans Langsdorff, obtained permission to stay for four days. The British, meanwhile, tried diplomacy to keep *Graf Spee* in harbor while they brought up naval reinforcements. By December 17, when the *Graf Spee* put to sea again, only HMS *Cumberland* had arrived, yet the anticipated battle never took place: Langsdorff, who believed a superior British force awaited him, had his crew scuttle the ship. Three days later, Langsdorff shot himself.

BATTLE OF THE RIVER PLATE

Location South Atlantic Ocean

Date December 13, 1939

Commanders and forces German: pocket battleship *Admiral Graf Spee* (Captain Langsdorff); British: cruisers *Exeter*, *Achilles*, and *Ajax* (Commodore Harwood)

Casualties German: 36 killed, 60 wounded; British: 72 killed, 28 wounded

Key actions After badly damaging HMS *Exeter* and scoring hits on HMS *Ajax*, Langsdorff, who had been wounded twice, ordered the lightly damaged pocket battleship *Admiral Graf Spee* to seek safety in the neutral port of Montevideo, Uruguay, instead of finishing off the British ships.

Key effects The scuttling of *Admiral Graf Spee* was the first real Allied success of the war, which had begun with the German defeat of Poland and then the start of the "phoney war." For his part, Adolf Hitler was predictably furious with Langsdorff's decision to destroy his own ship.

Rationing was introduced in Britain early in the New Year, but, as far as actual fighting was concerned, little happened in Western Europe until the spring. Elsewhere, the "Winter War" between the Soviet Union and Finland concluded in March 1940, and in the following month, Adolf Hitler issued orders for German forces to invade Denmark and Norway.

Denmark surrendered immediately, but the Norwegians fought on, with some British and French assistance. However, the German "Blitzkrieg" (meaning "lightning attack") through the Low Countries and into France in May 1940 meant that British and French troops were urgently needed there, and so their forces were reluctantly withdrawn from Norway. Norway was forced to surrender to the Nazis in June, once events in France meant that the Norwegians would have to continue fighting alone.

The German attack in the West

It was on May 10, 1940—which, coincidentally, was the same day that Winston Churchill replaced Neville Chamberlain as prime minister of Britain—that Germany invaded France, Belgium, and Holland. Germany's combination of fast armored tanks on land and superiority in the air made for a unified attacking force that was both innovative and effective. Despite greater numbers of air and army personnel—and the presence of the British Expeditionary Force—the forces of the Low Countries and France proved no match for Hitler's Wehrmacht and Luftwaffe. Holland and Belgium fell by the end of May; Paris, the French capital, was taken by German forces two weeks later.

British troops in northwestern France were forced to retreat from the German invaders in haste and withdrew to the Channel coast, where some 226,000 British and 110,000 French troops were eventually rescued from the French port of Dunkirk by a makeshift British fleet.

The German cruiser Königsberg *sinks in the harbour at Bergen, Norway, after a British air attack. Britain and France initially sent forces to aid Norway when it was invaded by Germany in April 1940, but, when Hitler launched his attack on Holland, Belgium, and France in May of the same year, the Allies were forced to withdraw their troops in order to confront the Nazi threat on the mainland of Western Europe.*

In France, an armistice was soon signed with Germany. The Nazis took direct control of the areas of northern France that they had occupied during their invasion, and they set up a puppet French government, based in Vichy, to control the "unoccupied" part of southern and eastern France. The Vichy government was placed under the nominal leadership of a French hero from World War I, Marshal Pétain.

Charles de Gaulle, as the leader of the Free French, fled to England to continue his country's fight against Hitler. However, it looked as though that fight might not last too long. Having conquered France, Hitler then turned his attention to Britain and began preparations for an invasion. However, for this to be successful, Hitler needed air superiority over the English Channel, and he charged the Luftwaffe with destroying British air power and coastal defenses, to pave the way for the seaborne invasion that Hitler codenamed Operation Sealion.

The Luftwaffe is defeated

The Battle of Britain, which lasted from July to September 1940, was the first to be fought solely in the air. Germany's Luftwaffe lacked warplanes, but had many skilled pilots. In Britain, the situation was reversed, but—crucially—the RAF also had radar. This significant advantage, combined with the fateful German decision to switch their air attacks away from airfields and factories to Britain's major cities, enabled the RAF to pull off a narrow but nonetheless remarkable victory. The triumph allowed the British to maintain air superiority over the English Channel and also ensured the (ultimately indefinite) postponement of Adolf Hitler's plans for the invasion of Britain. The victory of British, Commonwealth, and Allied pilots in defeating the onslaught from the Luftwaffe was to be the subject of one of Winston Churchill's greatest of all wartime speeches, in which he praised the men's bravery, memorably calling the triumph Britain's "finest hour."

Following the postponement of Hitler's invasion plans, however, came the "Blitz"—a sustained German bombing campaign against Britain's major cities that would last throughout the war. It would claim some 40,000 civilian lives and cause widespread devastation, but it did not break the spirit of the British people.

On April 9, 1940, a German invasion force composed of numerous surface ships, U-boats, and 1,000 aircraft attacked Denmark and Norway. Denmark was overrun immediately. The first ever airborne assault was made on Oslo and Stavanger airports in Norway, while ships landed troops at six locations. The Norwegian Army's six divisions had no tanks or effective artillery, while the country's coastal defenses and navy were generally weak. However, Norway's highly-motivated forces did score some successes. In Oslo Fjord, shore guns sank the German cruiser *Blücher*, claiming 1,600 lives. This successful attack enabled the Norwegian monarch King Haakon to escape northward with his government. Meanwhile, in the waters off Norway, the British battlecruiser HMS *Rodney* engaged the German battlecruisers *Scharnhorst* and *Gneisenau*, damaging the latter. In addition, the German cruiser *Karlsruhe* was sunk off Kristiansand by a British submarine.

After securing their initial objectives, the Germans began their conquest of Norway. However, they still faced some resistance. For example, Major General Carl Otto Ruge, Norway's new commander-in-chief, led a stubborn defense around Lake Mjösa and the Glomma Valley in central Norway.

On April 14, an Allied expeditionary force of more than 10,000 British, French, and Polish troops, which had been first formed to assist Finland, landed at Namsos, Alesund, and Narvik. Its objective was to recapture the port of Trondheim in order to secure a base in Norway, but its units were ill-prepared for the campaign, and there had been little liaison with the Norwegians. The various Allied units lacked cohesion, training in arctic warfare, key supplies, air cover, and antiaircraft weaponry.

German troops defended Trondheim strongly against the Allied assault and waited for the arrival of reinforcements, while German aircraft launched determined attacks against Allied positions. British and French troops eventually evacuated Namsos and Åndalsnes on May 1–2. Elsewhere, an Allied offensive on Narvik in northern Norway began with a naval bombardment. Allied coordination with the Norwegian forces was again poor, but the Germans in the area eventually withdrew at the end of April.

However, the German "Blitzkrieg" invasion of France and the Low Countries in May 1940 resulted in the Allies being forced to withdraw their troops from Norway at the beginning of June. The Norwegians then surrendered to the Germans on June 9, 1940.

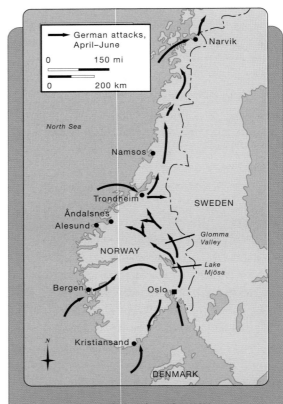

INVASION OF NORWAY

Location	Norway

Date	April 9–June 9, 1940

Commanders and forces German: 10,000 troops initially, rising to 100,000, 1,060 aircraft, and 24 warships (General Nikolaus von Falkenhorst); Norwegian: 12,000 troops plus 120,000 reservists, 102 aircraft (King Haakon). From April, the Norwegians were reinforced by 25,000 British and French troops, who were landed at Namsos, Åndalsnes and Narvik

Casualties German: 5,100; Norwegian: 850; British and French: 4,900

Key actions From April 9, German aircraft, flying from Norwegian and Danish bases, maintained air superiority over Norway and the Baltic Sea. This kept British warships away from German ships that were bringing in reinforcements, and also allowed the Luftwaffe to attack enemy troops in Norway itself. This greatly helped German ground forces in Norway.

Key effects Norwegian bases would prove useful for the Germans during the Battle of Britain, against the Soviet Union from 1941, and for attacks on Allied convoys to the Soviet Union. However, in the long term, Norway became a drain on German resources because Hitler continually reinforced the German occupying forces against a British invasion that never came.

On May 10, Germany's Army Group A, under General Gerd von Rundstedt, and Group B, commanded by General Fedor von Bock, invaded Holland and Belgium. Successful airborne landings were made against Belgium's key frontier fortress of Eben Emael, and also against targets in Holland. General Ritter von Leeb's Army Group C, meanwhile, engaged France's Maginot Line, the line of subterranean forts and other defensive positions along its border with Germany.

In accordance with Allied planning, British and French forces moved from France into Belgium to confront the German advance. This decision prompted Rundstedt to launch a surprise advance through the Ardennes, which eventually divided the Allied armies in Belgium from those in France. The Allied armies advanced into Belgium up to the Dyle and Meuse Rivers above Namur, a position known as the Dyle Plan Line, but were hampered by poor coordination with Dutch and Belgian forces.

In mid-May 1940, German forces reached the Meuse River, the crossing of which was critical for their advance into France. Dive-bombers pounded French positions, and inflatable rafts were used to establish bridgeheads at Sedan and Dinant on the 13th. Despite Allied air attacks, German armor advanced westward rapidly, opening a 50-mile (75-km) gap in the Allied line, and driving a wedge between the French Ninth and Second Armies, which then mounted a futile response.

German tanks reached Cambrai on May 18, and finally the coast at Abbeville two days later. It now became critical for the Allies to cut the "corridor" made by the panzers or risk the isolation of their armies to the north from their forces in the south. The dismissal of General Maurice Gamelin, the Allied commander-in-chief, and the appointment of Maxime Weygand as his successor on the 19th, further delayed military decision-making, which reduced the potential for any action.

Meanwhile, as British tanks battled the German 7th Panzer Division at Arras, General Heinz Guderian moved toward Boulogne and Calais unaffected by the Allied "Weygand Plan," which attempted to split the tank spearhead from troops and supplies in the German corridor. Boulogne and Calais capitulated soon after the naval evacuation of Allied troops.

Eager to preserve his panzers (tanks) for taking Paris, France, Hitler halted Rundstedt's armor at Gravelines and allowed his air force to attack the Allied pocket centering on Dunkirk. Operation Dynamo, the evacuation of Allied forces from the Dunkirk area, began on May 26. A defensive perimeter established on the Aa, Scarpe, and Yser "canal line" covered the withdrawal, while an assorted rescue flotilla of pleasure boats, commercial craft, and naval vessels crossed and recrossed the English Channel. The scene was now set for the German conquest of the rest of France.

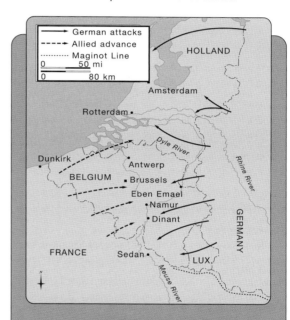

INVASION OF THE WEST

Location France, Belgium, and Holland

Date May 10–June 4, 1940

Commanders and forces German: 2,350,000 troops, 2,700 tanks, 3,200 aircraft (Adolf Hitler); Britain: 237,000 troops (General Lord Gort); French: 2 million troops (General Gamelin); Belgian: 375,000 troops (King Leopold III); Dutch: 250,000 troops (General Henri Gerard Winkelman). Total Allied tanks: 3,000. Total Allied aircraft: 1,700

Casualties German: 10,200 killed, 42,500 wounded, 8,400 missing; Allied: 150,000 killed and wounded, 1,200,000 captured

Key actions German victory at The Battle of Sedan on May 13-15 allowed 1,900 German tanks to exit the hilly Ardennes region of Belgium and strike west into the open plains of northern France. With the French and British armies lured north into Belgium and Holland to counter the German offensive, there was nothing to stop the Germans reaching the English Channel and cutting off the Allied armies from the rest of France.

Key effects The spectacular success of the German "Blitzkrieg" advance into the Low Countries and France in 1940 allowed the German Army to rapidly regroup for the last part of the campaign: the conquest of the whole of France.

BATTLE OF FRANCE

German motorized units make rapid progress in France in 1940.

On June 5, a German force of 119 divisions opened Operation Red, the conquest of France. French forces fought determined actions, but lacked manpower and equipment. On June 10, Italy declared war on France and Britain. Paris was declared an "open city" on June 13 to save it from destruction, and German troops entered the French capital on June 14.

French Prime Minister Paul Reynaud resigned and Marshal Henri-Philippe Pétain replaced him. Pétain requested Germany's armistice terms on June 17. After Italy's armistice with France on the 24th, a ceasefire occurred on all fronts. Germany then occupied two-thirds of France. The southern sector, known as Vichy France, was ruled by a puppet French government.

BATTLE OF FRANCE

Location France

Date June 5–21, 1940

Commanders and forces German: Army Group A (General von Rundstedt), Army Group B (General von Bock), Army Group C (General von Leeb); French: Army Group 2 (General Pretelat), Army Group 3 (General Besson), Army Group 4 (General Huntziger)

Casualties German: 95,000 killed and wounded; French: 150,000 killed and wounded, 800,000 taken prisoner

Key actions The attack by German Army Group B between June 5 and 13 destroyed the French Tenth Army and breached the French frontline. Despite heroic French resistance, especially by the Fourth Army, German victory was assured. Thereafter, the French armies disintegrated.

Key effects The fall of France left Adolf Hitler the master of continental Europe. He could now turn his focus to forcing Britain out of the war.

BATTLE OF BRITAIN

The Battle of Britain was Germany's attempt to gain air superiority over the skies of southern England. With this achieved, Germany could control the English Channel to enable the safe crossing of their invasion force (Operation Sealion), which was being prepared. Germany's air force commander, Hermann Göring, assembled 2,800 aircraft against Britain's 700 fighters. Widespread German attacks on ports, shipping, and airfields lured British fighters into action and they suffered heavy losses. Britain's fate now rested upon the bravery and skill of its fighter pilots. These men were drawn from the British Empire, North America, Czechoslovakia, Poland, and other Allied nations. The performance of the Hurricane and Spitfire fighters they flew also played a key role.

Crucially, Britain's centralized command-and-control and radar network enabled its fighters to be effectively concentrated to meet enemy attacks. Germany's gravest strategical error, however, was Hitler's decision, from September 7 onward, to concentrate on the bombing of British cities, despite having successfully eroded the capability of Britain's Fighter Command by constant raids across southern England. This change in strategy enabled the RAF to concentrate its fighters and to inflict heavier losses on the Luftwaffe. The RAF also benefited from longer flying time, as it operated over its own territory. In addition, crews who baled out were able to resume fighting, unlike their enemies, who parachuted into captivity.

"Eagle Day" on August 13 heralded a four-day German air offensive designed to destroy Britain's Fighter Command with raids on airfields and industrial targets. Göring postponed the early raids, however,

and later attacks on Britain by his Luftwaffe forces proved to be inconclusive.

On September 17, 1940, after Germany's failure to achieve aerial supremacy over southern England, Hitler suspended Operation Sealion.

BATTLE OF BRITAIN

Location Britain

Date July–September, 1940

Commanders and forces German: Air Fleet 2 (General Albert Kesselring), Air Fleet 3 (General Hugo Sperrle), Air Fleet 5 (General Hans-Jurgen Stumpff); British: Fighter Command (Air Chief Marshal Sir Hugh Dowding)

Total German air strength 2,800 aircraft

Total British fighter strength 715 plus 424 in storage

Casualties German aircraft lost: 1,733; British aircraft lost: 915

Key actions The crucial period of the Battle of Britain was between August 24 and September 15, 1940. Britain's Fighter Command came closest to defeat when its vital airfields around London were attacked. The decisive turning point came on September 7, when the German Luftwaffe switched its attention to the capital (in retaliation for British bombing raids on Berlin and other German cities). This tactical blunder by Hitler allowed Fighter Command to recover its strength rapidly to inflict losses significant enough to show the Germans the battle could not be won. On September 15, 56 German aircraft were shot down.

Key effects The Germans realized that the RAF could not be defeated in 1940. Germany was also preparing to attack the Soviet Union, so the plan to invade Britain, Operation Sealion, was cancelled indefinitely and eventually abandoned altogether. By the end of September 1940, the Battle of Britain was over. It was the first battle in history to be decided purely in the air and it was also the first real test of air power as both a defensive and an offensive weapon of war.

British pilots rush to their Hurricane fighter planes during the Battle of Britain in 1940.

Police and rescue workers clear debris after a German air raid on London. The Nazi bombings quickly spread to other British cities.

In late August 1940, the RAF launched a night raid on Berlin, Düsseldorf, Essen, and other German cities. The raids contributed toward a key change in German strategy, as aircraft were redirected to make retaliatory raids on London. Full-scale bombing raids on London—the "Blitz"—began on September 7, with 500 bombers and 600 fighters. German planes also targeted other British cities. The infamous raid of November 14, 1940, on Coventry saw 500 German bombers drop 500 tons of explosives and 900 incendiary bombs in 10 hours.

The main air offensive against British cities ended after May 1941, when Hitler turned his German war machine toward the Soviet Union. However, sporadic and lethal raids on Britain, using increasingly larger bombs, continued for several years.

THE BLITZ

Location Britain

Date September 7, 1940–May 11, 1941

Commanders and forces German: the Luftwaffe (Hermann Goering); British: RAF Fighter Command (Air Chief Marshal Sir Hugh Dowding)

Casualties German: 518 aircraft destroyed; British: 43,000 killed, 1.4 million made homeless

Key actions Because they could not continue with daylight raids on British factories, due to heavy aircraft losses, the Germans could not effectively target British war industries. Bombing British cities caused heavy civilian casualties, but it did not break the morale of the British people and, in fact, led to an increasingly united community spirit.

Key effects An undefeated Britain in the West in the spring of 1941 meant that Germany would be faced with a war on two fronts when Adolf Hitler's invasion of the Soviet Union (Operation Barbarossa) was launched in June 1941. In addition, heavy losses of skilled Luftwaffe aircrews over Britain would be keenly felt during Operation Barbarossa.

ITALIAN OFFENSIVE IN NORTH AFRICA

Italian dictator Benito Mussolini had ambitions to create an Italian empire around the Mediterranean Sea. When he came to power in 1924, Italy had several overseas possessions: Libya in North Africa, Eritrea and Italian Somaliland in East Africa, and the Dodecanese islands in the Mediterranean. Mussolini expanded his army and air force, and, in April 1930, he began a massive program of naval expansion.

In June 1940, Mussolini entered World War II on the German side. On September 13, 1940, an Italian force of 250,000 men under Marshal Rodolfo Graziani advanced from Libya into neighboring Egypt against the British Western Desert Force of two divisions under Major General Sir Richard O'Connor, the ultimate Italian aim being to seize the Suez Canal.

Having advanced 60 miles (100km) into Egypt, the Italian force halted to build fortified positions and to await supplies. Graziani established camps along a 50-mile (75-km) front, while the British remained 75 miles (120 km) to the east. British plans to attack Graziani were delayed, as many units had been redirected to Crete and Greece, where an Italian invasion was feared.

On December 9, General Sir Archibald Wavell, commander-in-chief in the Middle East and North Africa, launched the first British offensive in the Western Desert. Major General Sir Richard O'Connor's Western

Desert Force of 30,000 British and Commonwealth troops, supported by aircraft and long-range naval gunfire, was ordered to attack the fortified camps that had been established by the Italians in Egypt. Sidi Barrani was captured on the 10th and many Italian troops were taken prisoner as they retreated rapidly from Egypt.

ITALIAN OFFENSIVE IN NORTH AFRICA

Location North Africa

Date September 13, 1940–February 7, 1941

Commanders and forces British: Western Desert Force (Major General Richard O'Connor), 30,000 troops, 120 field guns, 275 tanks; Italian: Tenth Army (Marshal Rodolfo Graziani), 250,000 troops, 1,500 field guns, 300 tanks, 390 aircraft

Casualties British: 500 killed, 1,373 wounded; Italian: 130,000 prisoners

Key actions Following the Italian halt at Sidi Barrani on September 16, Graziani did nothing for the next two months. This allowed the British to organize a counterattack, which was launched on December 9. This attack smashed a hole in the Italian line of defenses. Assisted by aircraft and naval gunfire, the British expelled the Italians from Egypt and then made preparations to invade Libya.

Key effects The threatened Italian collapse in North Africa forced Adolf Hitler to send German forces to the region in order to bolster the Axis war effort. First to arrive there were 500 Luftwaffe aircraft, which launched bombing raids against Benghazi from bases in Sicily. Next came the tanks of the Afrika Korps under the command of Erwin Rommel, which landed in North Africa in March 1941. The war in North Africa would continue until 1943.

Italian forces invade Egypt from Libya in 1940. The offensive was later shattered by a British counterattack.

ITALY ATTACKS GREECE

TARANTO

Greek troops send letters home during the war against the Italian invasion in 1940. Greek forces eventually triumphed.

With no quick victory in sight in Africa, on October 28 Italy invaded Greece from Albania. Benito Mussolini hoped for a rapid advance, but mountainous terrain and winter weather hampered the operation. On November 14, Greece launched a major counterattack, and 3,400 British troops, plus air support, arrived from Egypt to aid the push. When Greek forces finally entered Koritza, they captured 2,000 Italians and drove the invaders back into Albania by December.

In early March 1941, Italy launched a spring offensive in northwest Greece, and Mussolini himself traveled to Albania to supervise the deployment of 12 divisions for the attack. Greek intelligence and defensive preparations ensured that the poorly-planned Italian attacks from Albania were rebuffed.

During the summer and early autumn of 1940, Britain's Royal Navy was facing great difficulties in the Mediterranean. The presence of the large Italian fleet at Taranto, based around six battleships, was a potent threat. The attack on this fleet by British Swordfish torpedo-bombers in a night operation was an outstanding success, and showed that capital ships, even in well-protected anchorages, were very vulnerable to aerial assault. Japanese observers in Italy were especially impressed, and they incorporated the lessons of the raid into the planning for their attack on the U.S. fleet at Pearl Harbor, which took place on December 7, 1941, and which was destined to be a major turning point in World War II

During the Taranto raid, some of the British Swordfish torpedo-bombers were armed with torpedoes, while others carried bombs. The torpedoes used were specially modified so that they could be effective in the shallow (40ft/12m) water of Taranto harbor. One Italian battleship was sunk and two other Italian battleships and two cruisers were damaged in the raid.

The successful British operation at Taranto forced the Italians to move their remaining battleships to safer, more distant naval bases on Italy's west coast, leaving the Mediterranean Sea open to the British. British warships were now free to support a major counterattack on the Italians in Egypt.

ITALIAN ATTACK ON GREECE

Location   Greece

Date   October 28, 1940–March 9, 1941

Commanders and forces   Italian: part of Ninth and Eleventh Armies (General Sebastiano Visconti Prasca), 163,000 troops; Greek: Greek Army (General Alexander Papagos), 150,000 troops

Casualties   Italian: 63,000 killed, 100,000 wounded, 23,000 taken prisoner; Greek: 13,000 killed, 42,000 wounded, 1,500 taken prisoner

Key actions   Mussolini never authorized the use of his navy or air force to assist in this attack. Also, the invasion coincided with the Greek rainy season when the weather dropped below freezing and many Italian soldiers did not possess winter boots. As a result, the Italians could make little headway against determined Greek counterattacks.

Key effects   Italy's failure resulted in Hitler having to invade Greece and Yugoslavia in April 1941 to secure his southern flank before he could invade the Soviet Union. The loss of time, troops, and vehicles would have major consequences for the Germans during the invasion of the USSR.

TARANTO

Location   Italy

Date   November 11–12, 1940

Commanders and forces   British: Mediterranean Fleet (Admiral Cunningham); Italian: Italian Fleet (Vice Admiral Inigo Campioni)

Casualties   British: 2 aircraft destroyed; Italian: the battleship *Conte di Cavour* was sunk and the battleships *Littorio* and *Caio Duilio* were heavily damaged. In addition, 2 Italian cruisers were badly damaged and 2 fleet auxiliaries were sunk

Key actions   The British plan called for their warplanes to attack in two waves about an hour apart.

Key effects   As a result of the strike, the Italians withdrew the bulk of their fleet farther north to Naples. The Taranto Raid changed many naval experts' thoughts regarding air-launched torpedo attacks. Prior to Taranto, many believed that deep water (100ft/30m) was needed to successfully drop torpedoes. To compensate for the shallow water of Taranto harbor (40ft/12m), the British specially modified their torpedoes and dropped them from very low altitude. This solution, as well as other aspects of the raid, was heavily studied by the Japanese as they planned their attack on the U.S. naval base at Pearl Harbor, which took place in December 1941.

With continental Europe under Nazi control following Germany's "Blitzkrieg" attacks of the first half of 1940, and Britain relatively safe for the time being, having withstood the onslaught of the Battle of Britain and the Blitz of fall 1940, in 1941 the war took on a more global dimension. Following the defeat of Italian fascist dictator Benito Mussolini's armies in Greece and at Tobruk, German forces arrived in North Africa in February 1941 and Adolf Hitler also ordered the invasion of Greece and Yugoslavia in April.

While the bombing of British and German cities continued, and the Nazi gas chambers at Auschwitz in Poland were put to use, Adolf Hitler then embarked on his next major operation and his most ambitious to date: the invasion of the Soviet Union. Operation Barbarossa, as the invasion was called, began on June 22, 1941.

The quest for "living space"

Operation Barbarossa had been delayed while German forces conquered Greece and Yugoslavia, but it was the military conquest of the Soviet Union in search of what Hitler called *lebensraum* or "living space" for the German people, that had long been the Führer's main aim. Barbarossa was directed against what was, in theory, a German ally. Under the nonaggression pact, signed in 1939, Germany and the Soviet Union had agreed not to attack or to support any act of aggression against one other. At the time, the pact had been mutually beneficial. It had allowed Hitler to concentrate his forces on invading and subduing Poland, without worrying about a Soviet attack; and it permitted the communist dictator, Joseph Stalin, to build up the Red Army to face any future threat from Hitler. The pact had also included secret clauses dividing eastern Europe; Poland would be split, the Balkans come into the German sphere of influence, and the Baltic nations would be under Soviet dominance.

With his aims in Poland and the Balkans now realized, Hitler felt that the summer of 1941 would be an excellent time to strike against the Soviet Union. The timing of his decision was also influenced by increasing

Triumphant German troops aboard a Soviet train in 1941. Logistics were an essential element for both sides on the Eastern Front.

tensions with Stalin, who had begun to demand more influence in the Balkans. Hitler justified his attack on the Soviet Union by claiming that Stalin was preparing to attack Nazi Germany, and, indeed, Stalin had been deploying large numbers of troops along his western borders. However, while some historians agree that Stalin intended an invasion of German territory, most consider that his measures were simply precautions against a possible Nazi attack.

The German invasion of the USSR

Barbarossa began well for Hitler. The initial advance was swift, with the fall of Sevastopol in Crimea being achieved at the end of October and the Soviet capital city of Moscow coming under attack at the end of the year. However, the bitter Russian winter (similar to the one that the French emperor Napoleon Bonaparte had experienced a century and a half earlier, when he had tried to conquer Russia) crippled the Nazi invasion force. The Soviet Red Army then launched a counterattack in December 1941, and the Eastern Front subsequently stagnated until the following spring.

Elsewhere in 1941, in the Mediterranean and the Atlantic, Britain and its allies continued to fight a bitter maritime war to protect their vital sea lanes against Germany's potent U-boat threat. The Battle of the Atlantic, in particular, was one which would continue until the end of the war.

The United States, meanwhile, was continuing to offer support to Britain in terms of supplies and war materials, but had not yet committed itself to the fight. This all changed on December 7, 1941, when the Japanese, tired of U.S. trade embargoes, mounted a surprise attack on the U.S. Navy base at Pearl Harbor, in Hawaii. U.S. president Franklin D. Roosevelt described it as "a date which will live in infamy" in a speech to Congress the following day. The U.S. Senate then voted unanimously to declare war on Japan.

This vote ensured that global conflict would now commence, with Germany declaring war on the United States a few days later. Within a week of Pearl Harbor, Japan had invaded the Philippines, Burma, and Hong Kong. The Pacific War was on, and the Allies now faced a long, bitter struggle on all fronts.

ITALIAN EAST AFRICA

Italy had large numbers of troops in the Italian territories of Ethiopia, Eritrea, and Italian Somaliland. These forces posed a threat to British territory to the west and south, and also to the Suez Canal.

On January 19, 1941, British forces in the Sudan, led by General William Platt, began attacking Italian forces, heralding the start of General Sir Archibald Wavell's campaign against Italian East Africa. Shortly afterward, on January 29, British forces in Kenya, led by General Sir Alan Cunningham, began attacking the Italian colony's garrison. By February 25, British-led troops had advanced into Mogadishu, the capital. The defeated Italians then began evacuating the colony.

The Battle of Keren (March 27), in northeast Eritrea, ended with Italian forces being forced to retreat toward the capital Asmara. The Italians lost 3,000 men; British fatalities were 536. Asmara fell five days later.

After an advance of 1,000 miles (1,600 km) from Kenya, Cunningham's forces captured Addis Ababa, Ethiopia's capital city, on April 6, and then continued to harass the retreating Italian forces. Allied forces in Eritrea seized the port of Massawa on the 9th and captured 17 Axis merchant vessels and other assorted craft in the harbor.

The Italians made their last major stand at the Battle of Amba Alagi (May 3) in northern Ethiopia. The rapid surrender of the Duke of Aosta and 7,000 troops marked Allied victory in East Africa. The Allied victory safeguarded the vital sea route through the Suez Canal in Egypt and also secured control of the Red Sea for use by Allied shipping.

ITALIAN EAST AFRICA

Location   Eritrea, Somaliland, and Ethiopia

Date   January 19–May 18, 1941

Commanders and forces   British: 70,000 troops, 100 aircraft (Lieutenant General Alan Cunningham and Lieutenant General William Platt); Italian: 100,000 troops, 103 tanks, 325 aircraft (Duke Amedeo of Aosta)

Casualties   British: 3,100 killed and wounded; Italian: 55,000 killed and wounded

Key actions   Platt's defeat of the Italians at Agordat on January 31 and Keren on March 27 cost Aosta 55,000 killed and wounded. These losses, combined with Cunningham's capture of Addis Ababa, resulted in the total collapse of the Italian war effort in East Africa.

Key effects   In a daring campaign, the British had eliminated any threat to the Suez Canal and had secured the Red Sea as an Allied supply route.

ROMMEL'S 1ST OFFENSIVE

German General Erwin Rommel began his first offensive in Libya on March 24 by driving the British from El Agheila. By April 4, Rommel's Axis troops were advancing across Libya in three groups. A mainly Italian force took Benghazi. Another was advancing to Msus, as was a third force farther south.

On April 10, Rommel began the siege of Tobruk. The Allies were determined to hold Tobruk as it was a strategic base for their forces fighting in North Africa. Tobruk came under constant air and ground attack, its caves providing the only real shelter, while the sea lane to Egypt was its only lifeline. On April 30, the most intense Axis attack on Tobruk began, but met stern resistance. Four days later, Axis forces secured a salient on the southwestern area of the defensive perimeter. Both sides then dug in for a long campaign, with the garrison dependent on supplies brought in by the Royal Navy. German submarines, torpedo-boats, and bombers constantly threatened the supply vessels.

On May 15, Operation Brevity, the first British operation against the Afrika Korps, attempted to throw the Axis forces back from the Egyptian frontier. Halfaya Pass and Sollum were recaptured in the operation. Rommel's offensive was effectively over.

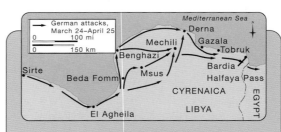

ROMMEL'S 1ST OFFENSIVE

Location   North Africa

Date   March 24–May 30, 1941

Commanders and forces   German: Afrika Korps (Major General Erwin Rommel); British: 2nd Armoured Division and 9th Australian Infantry Division, 3 Indian Motor Brigade, 50 aircraft (Lieutenant General Philip Neame)

Casualties   Unknown

Key actions   Rommel's failure to capture Tobruk meant that the Afrika Korps could not advance eastward into Egypt.

Key effects   Rommel's first offensive in North Africa was the beginning of the myth of the "Desert Fox." His boldness and willingness to always attack indicated that the war in North Africa would not be over quickly. In addition, the desert war was no longer one-sided: the British now faced a commander who led highly mobile and capable mechanized forces.

CAPE MATAPAN

In March 1941, the Italian fleet sailed into the Aegean Sea to disrupt British convoys to Greece. A British force led by Admiral Henry Pridham-Wippell quickly engaged some of the Italian cruisers in a long-range bombardment. The Italians retired, fearing the presence of more enemy vessels.

Their fears were realized when the main British force, consisting of Royal Navy warships *Formidable*, *Warspite*, *Barham*, and *Valiant*, led by Admiral Sir Andrew Cunningham, sent two torpedo-bombers from the carrier HMS *Formidable* to attack the Italian naval vessels. The planes damaged the Italian battleship *Vittorio Veneto* and crippled the cruiser *Pola*. Three British battleships then engaged two Italian cruisers that had been sent to try to protect the *Pola*. However, *Pola* was eventually sunk.

The Battle of Cape Matapan claimed five Italian ships sunk and around 2,400 men killed. The British lost just one aircraft in the action. The Italian Fleet never again ventured into the Eastern Mediterranean.

CAPE MATAPAN

Location Aegean Sea

Date March 28, 1941

Commanders and forces British: Mediterranean Fleet (Admiral Cunningham, 1 aircraft carrier, 3 battleships, 15 cruisers); Italian: Italian Fleet (Admiral Iachino, 1 battleship, 8 cruisers)

Casualties British: 1 aircraft lost, 3 aircrew killed; Italian: 5 ships lost, 2,400 sailors killed

Key actions Late in the day on March 28, the Italian naval commander, Admiral Iachino, ordered two cruisers and four destroyers to go the aid of the stricken cruiser *Pola*. This allowed Admiral Cunningham's Royal Navy ships to close with the Italian vessels and engage them in a night battle. As a result, the Italians lost five ships sunk, with the loss of 2,400 sailors.

Key effects The defeat at Cape Matapan dealt another crushing blow to the Italian Navy's morale as much as to its fleet of warships.

The Italian battleship Vittorio Veneto *fires a massive salvo against Royal Navy warships in the Aegean Sea during the Battle of Cape Matapan in March 1941. The Italian ship was hit by British torpedo-bombers during the engagement. Despite taking on several thousand tons of water due to the extensive torpedo damage,* Vittorio Veneto *was able to reach the safe haven of the Italian port at Taranto, but the battleship remained out of active service for the next five months.*

German parachutists engaged in street fighting with Allied forces in Corinth during the German invasion of Greece.

In April 1941, 33 German divisions, along with Italian and Hungarian support, invaded Yugoslavia from the north, east, and southeast. Aerial bombing centered on the capital, Belgrade, dislocated Yugoslavia's military command and communications structure, and hampered the mobilization of its army. Major cities were quickly seized, including Zagreb, Belgrade, and Sarajevo, between the 10th and 15th. On April 17, Yugoslavia signed an armistice with Germany. However, local guerrilla forces quickly formed to launch a campaign of resistance against the Nazi occupation.

In Greece, German forces attacked the Greek Second Army on the fortified Metaxas Line along the country's northern border with Bulgaria. Air raids on the port of Piraeus destroyed a British ammunition ship, which exploded, sinking 13 other vessels nearby. The Second Army, cut off after German forces reached the sea at Salonika on the 9th, soon surrendered. The British, after initially occupying positions between Mount Olympus and Salonika, were forced back to a new defensive line just north of the mountains, after the collapse of Greek forces on their left flank.

By April 18, Greek positions were collapsing as the German invaders advanced. The British fell back from Mount Olympus to Thermopylae. A British evacuation appeared inevitable as reinforcements from Egypt were canceled on the 18th. King George assumed temporary charge of the Greek government after the premier,

Alexander Koryzis, killed himself. A British evacuation was finalized after Greek commander-in-chief Marshal Alexander Papagos saw the situation was hopeless and recommended a withdrawal on the 21st. Greek forces fighting in Albania surrendered on the 20th.

British forces left their lines around Thermopylae on the 24th, after Greek forces in Thrace capitulated to the Nazis. Some 43,000 men were rescued by the Royal Navy from ports and beaches in eastern Greece, while under constant German air attack.

An aerial assault by German paratroopers at Corinth on the 26th and an advance to Patras posed a significant threat to the British evacuation. German forces occupied the Greek capital, Athens, on the 27th, but the Greek government had already left for Crete.

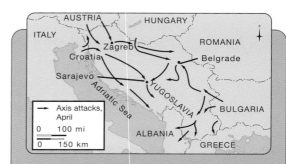

GREECE & YUGOSLAVIA

Location Greece and Yugoslavia

Date April 6–27, 1941

Commanders and forces German: Second Army (General von Weichs), Twelfth Army (Field Marshal von List); Total German forces: 680,000 troops, 1,200 tanks, 700 aircraft. Italian: Second Army (General Vittorio Ambrosio, 565,000 troops). Yugoslavian: Yugoslav Army (King Peter II, 1 million men, 700 aircraft). Greek: Greek Army (Marshal Alexander Papagos, 430,000 troops, 50 aircraft). British: 62,000 troops, 100 tanks, 200 aircraft (Field Marshal Henry Maitland Wilson)

Casualties German: 5,600; Yugoslav: 100,000 killed and wounded, 300,000 captured; Greek: 70,000 killed and wounded, 270,000 captured; British: 11,840 killed and wounded, 7,000 captured, 200 aircraft destroyed

Key actions In Yugoslavia, heavy German air attacks on Belgrade paralyzed the enemy high command, while German ground attacks from the north, east, and southeast sliced through poorly equipped Yugoslav forces. In Greece in the first three days, the Germans penetrated the Metaxas Line, forcing the surrender of the entire Greek Second Army. This allowed the German panzers to get through the mountains of northern Greece and into the center of the country.

Key effects Although it was a stunning success, the Balkan campaign delayed two panzer divisions from joining the invasion of the Soviet Union in June 1941. In addition, the German Army was forced to deploy forces to guard the long coastlines of Yugoslavia and Greece, and in central Yugoslavia to try to combat partisan guerrilla groups.

BATTLE FOR CRETE

On May 20, 1941, a German assault force, supported by 500 aircraft, attacked the Greek island of Crete as part of an airborne assault that would then be reinforced by a seaborne force. After preparatory air attacks, the Germans launched the first major airborne operation in history.

Paratroops came under immediate attack while landing and met determined resistance from the 42,000 British, New Zealand, Australian, and Greek troops stationed on the island. After an Allied battalion commander who was defending Máleme airfield mistakenly withdrew, the Germans gained a footing for reinforcements to be landed. While the Germans were able to land some troops by glider and parachute, around 5,000 men were lost on vessels sailing from Greece that were intercepted by British ships. The British Mediterranean Fleet in Cretan waters was subjected to massive German air attacks on the 22nd, forcing it to withdraw its ships off northern Crete.

Major General Bernard Freyberg, the New Zealand commander responsible for defending Crete, decided on May 28 that the island could not be saved, as the German offensive had intensified and his forces were already retreating toward Sfakia on the south coast. The Royal Navy's hazardous naval evacuation saved over 15,000 Allied troops, but it lost nine ships in the process. Hitler suspended further airborne operations on a similar scale after being informed of the devastating losses suffered by his paratroopers on Crete.

BATTLE FOR CRETE

Location Crete

Date May 20–31, 1941

Commanders and forces German: XI Air Corps (General Kurt Student, 10,000 troops, 500 aircraft), VIII Air Corps (610 fighters and bombers); British: 27,500 British and Commonwealth troops, plus 14,000 Greeks (Major General Bernard Freyberg)

Casualties German: 7,000 killed and wounded; British: 17,000 killed and wounded, plus 11,800 taken prisoner

Key actions The key to winning the battle was the German capture of Máleme airfield. On May 21, paratroopers captured the vital Hill 107, due to a mistaken withdrawal by its New Zealand defenders. Thereafter, the Germans were able to land reinforcements on the airfield.

Key effects In mid-July 1941, Adolf Hitler informed General Student that the high losses on Crete meant that the day of the large-scale air assault was over. As a result, Germany would make no more air assaults of this size throughout the remainder of the war.

BATTLE OF THE DENMARK STRAIT

German battleship Bismarck *fires at the British warship HMS* Hood. *The* Hood *was sunk in the fierce battle in the Denmark Strait.*

In spring 1941, the German Navy (the Kriegsmarine) sank 22 allied ships in two months in the North Atlantic. For the next raid, Germany's newest battleship, the *Bismarck*, was escorted by the heavy cruiser *Prinz Eugen*. On May 21, the ships arrived in Norway, but were seen by a British Spitfire. The next day, the ships headed for the Denmark Strait, between Iceland and Greenland. Two British cruisers, *Norfolk* and *Suffolk*, located *Bismarck* and *Prinz Eugen* there on May 22.

Next day, the German ships sank the British battlecruiser HMS *Hood*. *Bismarck*'s oil tanks, however, were hit and began to leak. The German vessels escaped, and the British lost radar contact for several hours. Aircraft from HMS *Ark Royal* disabled *Bismarck*'s steering with a torpedo on the 26th and other British ships encircled her. Shelling from HMS *Rodney* and HMS *King George V* did great damage, and the *Bismarck* eventually sank on May 27.

BATTLE OF THE DENMARK STRAIT

Location Denmark Strait, North Atlantic

Date May 23–27, 1941

Commanders and forces German: Battleship *Bismarck*, heavy cruiser *Prinz Eugen* (Vice Admiral Lütjens); British: heavy cruisers *Suffolk* and *Norfolk*, aircraft carrier *Ark Royal*, battleships *Rodney*, *King George V*, and *Prince of Wales*, battlecruiser *Hood* (Vice Admiral Holland)

Casualties German: 1,995; British: 1,500

Key actions Though *Bismarck* sank the *Hood* and damaged the *Prince of Wales*, shells from the latter damaged the German battleship, leaving it listing to port, down at the bow, and unable to use all its oil fuel. Its maximum speed, seafaring ability, and range were all reduced. This allowed British ships to catch it on May 26. *Bismarck* sank on May 27, after a night battle.

Key effects Following the loss of the *Bismarck*, the Germans abandoned the use of heavy surface warships for raiding purposes in the Atlantic. From then on, the Germans concentrated their efforts on the U-boat war.

INVASION OF SYRIA

On June 8, an Allied force of 20,000 Free French, British, and Commonwealth troops under the command of General Sir Henry M. Wilson invaded Syria in the eastern Mediterranean, advancing from Palestine and Iraq, amid fears of increasing German influence in Syria. The Allied force faced 35,000 Vichy French troops under the command of General Henri Dentz, plus naval forces that engaged the Allies on the 9th.

In subsequent days, the Allies encircled enemy units and used heavy artillery to overcome resistance. Vichy forces abandoned the capital, Damascus, to the Allies on June 21.

On July 14, 1941, Dentz defied the Vichy French authorities and surrendered Syria to the Allies. British forces then began occupying the colony and pro-Allied administrations were formed in Syria and in neighboring Lebanon. These regimes, in turn, provided added protection to British-controlled Palestine and Egypt.

INVASION OF SYRIA

Location   Syria

Date   June 8–July 14, 1941

Commanders and forces   British and Commonwealth: 6th British Division (part), 7th Australian Division, 5th Indian Brigade, Free French units (General Henry Maitland Wilson), 20,000 troops; Vichy French: 35,000 troops (General Henri Dentz)

Casualties   British and Commonwealth: 3,900 killed and wounded; Vichy French: 3,300 killed and wounded, plus 3,000 captured

Key actions   Despite Vichy forces being well armed with machine guns, mortars, artillery, and aircraft, Allied forces mounted continuous attacks that wore down the French, exhausting their reserves and forcing their eventual surrender.

Key effects   Allied control of Syria was secure, thus increasing the security of Palestine and Egypt.

OPERATION BATTLEAXE

General Sir Archibald Wavell launched Operation Battleaxe to relieve Tobruk and break the German hold on Cyrenaica in North Africa. An armored and infantry division crossed the Egyptian–Libyan border around Halfaya Pass, Fort Capuzzo, and Hafid Ridge. However, the new British tanks brought in to strengthen the 7th Armoured Division suffered mechanical problems and their crews had inadequate training. The weak Allied divisions suffered heavily against the experienced German armor and antitank guns. Wavell halted Operation Battleaxe after losing 100 of his tanks.

OPERATION BATTLEAXE

Location   North Africa

Date   June 15–17, 1941

Commanders and forces   German: 13,000 troops, plus 170 tanks and 210 aircraft (General Erwin Rommel); British: 20,000 troops, plus 200 tanks and 203 aircraft (General Sir Archibald Wavell)

Casualties   German: 700 killed and 70 tanks destroyed; British: 900 killed and 100 tanks destroyed

Key actions   On the first day, June 15, German 88mm antitank guns knocked out dozens of British tanks as they attacked Halfaya Pass. This effectively decided the outcome of the offensive.

Key effects   The morale of the Afrika Korps soared, while British spirits sank. Winston Churchill relieved Wavell of his command on June 21. Wavell was replaced by General Sir Claude Auchinleck.

Italian troops in action near Benghazi during the major British offensive in Cyrenaica, Libya.

OPERATION BARBAROSSA

On June 22, Hitler launched Operation Barbarossa, his invasion of the Soviet Union, aiming to achieve a speedy victory and destroy the Soviet Red Army before the summer ended, and also before the Soviets could

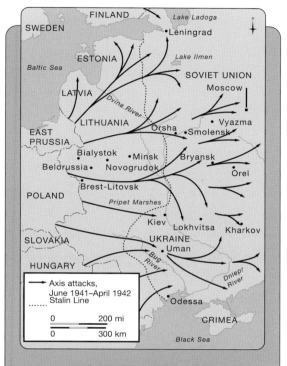

OPERATION BARBAROSSA

Location USSR

Date June 22–September 30, 1941

Commanders and forces German: Army of Norway (General Nikolaus von Falkenhorst), Army Group North (Field Marshal Wilhelm von Leeb), Army Group Center (Field Marshal Fedor von Bock), Army Group South (Field Marshal Gerd von Rundstedt); Finnish Army (Marshal Carl Mannerheim)

Force levels German: 3 million troops, 3,350 tanks, 7,200 field guns, 2,770 aircraft

Commanders and forces Soviet: Northern Front (General Popov), Northwestern Front (General Kuznetsov), Western Front (General Pavlov), Southwestern Front (General Kirponos), Southern Front (General Tiulenev), Reserve (six armies and four mechanized corps)

Force levels Soviet: 5.5 million troops, 24,000 tanks, 9,500 aircraft

Casualties German: 680,000; Soviet: 2.8 million

Key actions The German Blitzkrieg destroyed hundreds of Soviet aircraft on the ground in the first few days of Operation Barbarossa, and the speed of the German tank advance created vast pockets of trapped Soviet armies, at Bialystok, Minsk, Smolensk, Uman, and Kiev. At Kiev alone, in September 1941, 665,000 Red Army troops were killed or captured by German forces.

Key effects The decision by Adolf Hitler to divert armored forces from Army Group Center south to destroy Soviet forces in the Ukraine in July fatally delayed the advance on Moscow, the Soviet capital. This would have disastrous consequences in the fall and winter of 1941.

mobilize their immense industrial resources to resupply their army and air force. Soviet forces were caught by surprise by the German attack and quickly lost a series of battles along their frontier. In addition, German air attacks quickly destroyed 1,800 Soviet aircraft that were still on the ground. The German invasion force made rapid progress in the north and center of its advance, but met stiff resistance in the south.

By mid-July 1941, following the crossing of the Dniepr and Dvina rivers, the encirclement of Smolensk by Germany's Army Group Center commenced. The city fell after 300,000 Red Army troops and 3,200 Soviet tanks became trapped in the vicinity of the city. Despite this, the surrounded Soviet forces were not finally defeated until August.

On July 22, Germany's Army Group North halted west of Lake Ilmen, south of the city of Leningrad. Troops and equipment along the entire front were suffering from the rigors of the German advance and the stronger Soviet resistance that was now being encountered. During lulls in the fighting, the Soviets doggedly reinforced their defense lines, especially those that lay in front of the capital, Moscow, and Leningrad. Two days later, Adolf Hitler ordered Army Group South in the Ukraine to close the pocket around the concentration of Soviet forces based on Uman. They sealed it 15 days later, isolating three Soviet armies from Red Army forces that were positioned around Kiev. The Germans had trapped some 100,000 Soviet troops and 317 tanks in the pocket. This German success left the Soviet South and Southwest Fronts seriously weakened, and the key Black Sea port of Odessa was now only accessible by sea.

In mid-August 1941, Soviet forces in the Ukraine began withdrawing across the strategically-important Dniepr River to form a defensive line farther north—known as the Bryansk Front—leaving the Soviet Thirty-fifth Army in the city of Kiev.

Hitler wanted to trap and destroy the Soviet Red Army before it could cross the Dniepr, but the plan failed and Red Army troops were able to escape east. However, the Germans did capture the city of Kiev on September 19, killing or capturing 665,000 men after 40 days of bloody combat.

OPERATION TYPHOON

Operation Typhoon, the German attack on Moscow, officially began on September 30, when General Heinz Guderian's Second Panzer Group thrust toward Bryansk and Orel. Two days later, the German 3rd and 4th Panzer Groups moved to encircle Soviet forces around Vyazma. On October 6, Germany's Second Army and Second Panzer Army encircled three Soviet armies north and south of Bryansk. By the 14th, six Soviet armies were encircled at Vyazma. German forces elsewhere covered great distances, but the onset of heavy rains on October 8 severely limited mobility, as the roads to Moscow quickly become quagmires.

The German encirclements at Vyazma and Bryansk trapped 673,000 Soviet troops and numerous tanks, but the operations also preoccupied the advancing forces, giving the Red Army time to establish new defensive positions further back.

By mid-November 1941, the strength, mobility, morale, and logistical support of the German forces on the Eastern Front were severely affected by fierce winter weather. By the 27th, the panzer spearheads were only 20 miles (32 km) from the Soviet capital, Moscow, but the second phase of the German advance was soon halted by Soviet counterattacks and hampered by freezing temperatures. Red Army troops, many newly equipped with the superb T-34 tank and Katyusha multiple rocket-launchers, were also properly clothed for winter operations. Adolf Hitler suspended the German advance on Moscow on December 8.

OPERATION TYPHOON

Location   USSR

Date   September 30–December 8, 1941

Commanders and forces   German: Army Group Center (Field Marshal von Bock) 1,929,000 troops, 14,000 artillery pieces, 1,000 tanks, and 1,390 aircraft. Soviet: Western Front (General Konev), Reserve Front (General Budenny), Bryansk Front (General Eremenko) In total, the Red Army mustered 1,250,000 troops, 7,600 artillery pieces, 990 tanks, and 670 aircraft.

Casualties   German: 250,000; Soviet: 650,000

Key actions   In mid-November 1941, Soviet leader Joseph Stalin learned that Japan would not attack the Soviet Union in eastern Siberia. This information allowed him to deploy 100,000 troops from the eastern Soviet Union to the Moscow Front to confront the German invasion force, which by this time was grinding to halt due to a lack of supplies and the increasingly severe winter weather.

Key effects   The end of the Germans' Operation Typhoon in December 1941 marked the beginning of a Soviet counteroffensive all along the Eastern Front. This would eventually drive the German Army from the gates of Moscow. It would not return.

Soviet infantry in their winter clothing. German troops often lacked the kit to cope with the freezing temperatures on the Eastern Front.

OPERATION CRUSADER

South African troops use a grenade to clear Germans from a building during Operation Crusader, the attempt to relieve Tobruk.

The British Eighth Army in Egypt, under General Sir Alan Cunningham, launched Operation Crusader to relieve Tobruk by striking into Cyrenaica. British light tanks suffered serious losses (exacerbated by mechanical and tactical shortcomings) in various engagements with the Germans around Sidi Rezegh, southeast of Tobruk, from November 19 to 23.

On the 22nd, the Tobruk garrison attacked besieging Italian units in order to link up with the Eighth Army advancing to relieve it. General Erwin Rommel then struck at the Allied flank, but sustained heavy losses. He eventually retreated, relieving the pressure on Tobruk, although the fighting continued. On the 26th, General Neil Ritchie relieved Cunningham.

OPERATION CRUSADER

Location   North Africa

Date   November 18, 1941–January 31, 1942

Commanders and forces   German: Germany: Panzergruppe Afrika (General Erwin Rommel), 100,000 troops, 410 tanks, 320 aircraft; British: Eighth Army (Lieutenant General Alan Cunningham), 150,000 troops, 700 tanks, 1,000 aircraft

Casualties   German: 33,000 men and 300 tanks; British: 18,000 men and 278 tanks

Key actions   Despite some early German successes in tank battles that were waged around Sidi Rezegh, the situation was saved for the Allies by the advance of the British 13th Corps, which began engaging enemy positions along the coast on November 22; by November 26, 1941, 13th Corps' New Zealand Division had cleared a corridor between Tobruk and 30th Corps.

Key effects   The Allied operation had saved the vital Suez Canal from falling into German hands.

PEARL HARBOR

On December 7, 1941, a Japanese force attacked the U.S. Pacific Fleet at Pearl Harbor on Hawaii. Japanese aircraft sank three battleships and damaged or sank 21 other vessels, and killed more than 3,000 U.S. servicemen. Japan then declared war on the United States and the British Commonwealth.

Despite the attack's success, the U.S. Pacific Fleet's aircraft carriers were at sea and thus survived, while the fleet itself was quickly repaired. In the United States there was outrage over the attack and popular support for President Roosevelt's call for war on Japan.

PEARL HARBOR

Location   Oahu, Hawaii

Date   December 7, 1941

Commanders and forces   U.S.: Pacific Fleet (Admiral Husband Kimmel, 70 warships and 24 auxiliaries), U.S. Army (General Walter Short). Total number of U.S. aircraft: 300; Japanese: Carrier Striking Task Force (Vice Admiral Chuichi Nagumo, 5 aircraft carriers, 4 cruisers, 9 destroyers, 3 submarines, 423 aircraft)

Casualties   U.S.: 3 battleships sunk; in total 21 vessels sunk or damaged, 3,000 navy personnel killed, 876 wounded, 226 army personnel killed, and 396 wounded, 200 aircraft destroyed; Japanese: 29 aircraft destroyed, 5 midget submarines lost

Key actions   Strict radio silence allowed the Japanese fleet to approach Hawaii undetected and to achieve total surprise in the attack on December 7. On the day of the attack, the U.S. battleships in Pearl Harbor were not protected by antisubmarine nets, there were no barrage balloons over the harbor, and there was no equipment to put up a smoke screen over the anchored ships.

Key effects   The damage to the U.S Pacific Fleet was not fatal. All three fleet carriers were absent from Pearl Harbor on the day of the attack. The surprise attack outraged the U.S. public, who rallied behind their government. The United States had now entered World War II, and would become a military and economic giant in the next four years.

U.S. warships ablaze after the Japanese attack on Pearl Harbor, Hawaii, on December 7, 1941.

U.S. SUBMARINE CAMPAIGN

The Japanese attack on Pearl Harbor resulted in a significant although temporary loss of strength for the U.S. Navy. However, the only weapon system immediately available to take the war to the enemy was the U.S. Submarine Force. The impact that U.S. submarine forces had on the outcome of the war in the Pacific is often underestimated compared to that of the U.S. carrier force. The modernization of the world's navies in the World War II era certainly saw a shift from dependence on the battleship toward the aircraft carrier. However, the contribution of the U.S. Submarine Force was just as vital.

Comprising less then 1.6 percent of all U.S. naval personnel in the Pacific, yet accounting for more than half of all enemy shipping sunk, the U.S. submarine fleets were very important in the Allied effort for achieving victory. Historians believe that a major factor contributing to Japan's surrender in 1945 was Japan's recognition of the fact that it was unable to sustain the war effort due to the severe shortages of raw materials and basic essentials. By eliminating Japan's ability to import vital goods and supplies, U.S. submarines were able to do to Japan what Adolf Hitler's U-boat force ultimately failed to do to Britain, which was to cut its maritime lifeline.

U.S. SUBMARINE CAMPAIGN

Location Pacific Ocean

Date December 1941–August 1945

Forces and commanders U.S.: Submarine Force Pacific, 288 submarines (Vice Admiral Charles Lockwood); Japanese: Combined Fleet, 166 warships, 68 submarines (Admiral Isoroku Yamamoto). Merchant fleet, 2,337 ships

Casualties U.S.: 52 submarines; Japanese: 5.6 million tons of shipping

Key actions In August 1942, U.S. submarines were fitted with radar, which increased their chances of locating Japanese ships. In mid-1943, U.S. torpedoes were fitted with a more effective detonator mechanism, which meant that when they hit a ship they always exploded. This increased the number of Japanese ships sunk.

Key effects Comprising less then 1.6 percent of all U.S. naval personnel in the Pacific theater, yet accounting for more than half of all enemy shipping sunk, the U.S. submarine fleet made a critical contribution to the Allied victory over Japan. Merchant marine losses crippled the ability of Japanese industry to generate military equipment and armaments. Similarly, the sustained destruction of Japanese naval forces significantly reduced the Japanese ability to project their military power throughout the vast Pacific theater of war. Finally, the deployment of its submarine force enabled the U.S. Navy to take the offensive in Japanese-controlled waters and to inflict disproportionate losses relative to the number of U.S. submarines that were available.

MALAYA

A Japanese force of 100,000 troops (the 5th and 18th Divisions), under General Tomoyukai Yamashita, began landing on the northeast coast of Malaya and in Thailand after initial air attacks on December 8. Japanese units quickly moved southward down both sides of the Malayan Peninsula. British forces were mainly stationed in the south, having anticipated an attack nearer Singapore.

Japanese aircraft soon destroyed most of the British aircraft, and British reluctance to move into neutral Thailand before a Japanese attack enabled General Yamashita to complete his landings. British forces finally advanced into Thailand on the 10th, but could not halt the Japanese invasion. Well-equipped and experienced Japanese troops continued pushing southward, many by bicycle.

In early January 1942, British, Indian, and Australian forces began their retreat toward Singapore, as they were unable to mount any meaningful defense against the well-trained and well-equipped Japanese invaders. Kuala Lumpur, the Malaysian capital city, fell to the Japanese on January 12.

By the end of January 1942, British and Allied forces had been pushed back into Singapore, having abandoned the whole of the Malayan Peninsula, where mobile Japanese units had constantly outwitted them. In Singapore, the Allies awaited their fate.

MALAYA

Location Malaya

Date December 8, 1941–February 6, 1942

Commanders and forces British: Malaya Command (Lieutenant General Percival), 100,000 troops, 158 aircraft; Japanese: Twenty-Fifth Army (Lieutenant General Tomoyukai Yamashita), 100,000 troops, 568 aircraft, 200 tanks

Casualties British: 10,500 killed and wounded, 40,000 taken prisoner; Japanese: 4,200 killed and wounded

Key actions British and Allied troops had not been trained for jungle warfare, whereas the Japanese had been. This meant that the Japanese continually outflanked and infiltrated British positions. In addition, the Japanese made a number of amphibious landings from the sea to penetrate behind British lines.

Key effects As 1941 drew to a close, the British and their allies were pushed south toward their naval base in Singapore by the invading Japanese. They were demoralized, whereas Japanese morale was high. In addition, Japanese aircraft had sunk the British battleship *Prince of Wales* and battlecruiser *Repulse* on December 10, further weakening the British war effort in and around Malaya.

A Filipino family flees from their home with whatever they can take with them, following a Japanese bombardment. Thousands of civilians were affected by the fighting in the Philippine Islands.

At the beginning of their Philippine campaign, Japanese air attacks destroyed 100 U.S. aircraft at Clark Field, while a small force landed on Luzon Island to build an airfield there. General Douglas MacArthur, commanding the 130,000-strong U.S. and Filipino force in the Philippines, had intended that U.S. aircraft would strike the invading Japanese force, as his ground troops were not capable of preventing any landing. On the 10th, Luzon was invaded and Guam Island quickly fell. The Japanese forces also attacked Wake Island and captured it on the 24th, after two invasion attempts.

Japanese forces next invaded Mindanao, the most southerly island, and Jolo. The islands offered Japan the chance to gain naval and air bases. General MacArthur decided not to defend Manila, the capital, but declared it an open city in order to withdraw his forces westward to the Bataan Peninsula. MacArthur realized that Japan had air and sea superiority, and he also knew that no reinforcements would be sent to his aid. His troops began a desperate resistance against Japanese

attacks across the mountainous peninsula, which began on January 9, 1942. For several months, the U.S.-led force resisted the Japanese, despite suffering from tropical diseases and being short of supplies.

On April 3, Japan launched its final offensive on Bataan, beginning with air and artillery bombardments, and the U.S. line of defense was penetrated on the 4th. Major General Jonathan Wainright, commanding the U.S. and Filipino forces, could not mount an effective counterattack with his decimated units and the majority of his forces surrendered on April 9. The remaining U.S. and Filipino forces on Corregidor finally surrendered to the Japanese on May 6.

FALL OF THE PHILIPPINES

Location   Luzon, Philippines

Date   December 8, 1941–May 6, 1942

Commanders and forces   U.S.: U.S. Army Forces Far East, 130,000 troops, 120 aircraft (General Douglas MacArthur); Japanese: Fourteenth Army, 43,000 troops, 200 aircraft (Lieutenant General Masaharu Homma)

Casualties   U.S.: 2,000 killed and wounded, 11,500 taken prisoner; Japanese: 4,000 killed

Key actions   On December 8, Japanese air attacks destroyed more than half of the U.S. aircraft. On December 22, Japanese amphibious landings in the Lingayen Gulf forced General Douglas MacArthur to withdraw his forces to the island's Bataan Peninsula. This meant that the Americans were effectively under siege until they surrendered on May 6, 1942.

Key effects   The fight for Bataan forced the Japanese to commit more troops than planned to capture an objective far less important than Malaya or the Dutch East Indies.

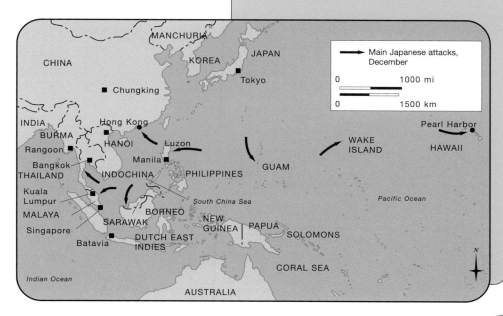

The **Japanese attack** on the U.S. naval base at Pearl Harbor, Hawaii, on December 7, 1941, was just the start of Japan's campaign of conquest in the Pacific. Japanese commanders unleashed a rapid onslaught against Allied forces in Asia to secure a string of impressive military victories. Japan took control of Thailand and northern Malaya and, on December 25, 1941, Japanese forces captured the British-held island of Hong Kong.

The British defense of Malaya ended on January 31, 1942, when the last British troops crossed the Johor Strait to Singapore. The defeat had cost many thousands killed or captured. Worse was to come for the British, when Japan began its assault on the island of Singapore on the night of February 8–9. Over the next few days, vicious, close-quarter fighting ensued. On February 11, Japanese troops captured and cut off the island's water supply. In a major defeat, the British commander, Lieutenant General Arthur Percival, was forced to surrender Singapore to Japan on February 15. Many thousands of British and Allied personnel were taken into captivity, many of whom would not survive the inhumane conditions under which they were held over the next few years.

Japanese conquests

Japan's conquests continued. In April, the Bataan Peninsula fell to Japan, as U.S. forces were driven from the Philippines and, in May, Japanese forces took Mandalay in Burma as British units were forced to withdraw to India. The Pacific islands of Sumatra, Borneo, and the Dutch East Indies fell to Japan as the Dutch and British colonial empires in the Pacific collapsed. In air, sea, and land warfare, the Imperial Japanese forces had proved far superior to their enemies. In particular, Japan had mastered the art of amphibious warfare, developing equipment and tactics for landing forces from the sea to provide rapid striking capability across the Pacific theater.

The Japanese conquests of the first half of 1942 stunned the Allies, and they quickly realized that they

An aerial photograph of the Japanese aircraft carrier Hiryu *during the Battle of Midway in June 1942. The ship was set ablaze by a U.S. air attack and was subsequently scuttled.*

faced a formidable foe. They particularly misjudged Japan's most potent weapon—its fleet of aircraft carriers. By June 1942, Japanese expansion in the Pacific had reached its height, but, during that month, the pendulum began to swing in the other direction. The Battle of Midway, in which U.S. sea-based aircraft destroyed four Japanese aircraft carriers, marked a major turning point in the Pacific War.

In Britain, U.S. troops began to arrive in preparation for an eventual Allied invasion of France. Meanwhile, the bombing campaign on major cities intensified in both England and Germany, with the first thousand-bomber Allied air raid on Cologne, Germany. In the Atlantic, the United States also began to experience the horrors of the U-boat war with attacks on the East Coast and in the Gulf of Mexico. However, due to rapid developments in antisubmarine technology, such as improved radar and depth-charge weaponry, German U-boat losses began to increase by the end of the year.

German defeats in North Africa and the USSR

In North Africa, Field Marshal Erwin Rommel's Afrika Korps began a counteroffensive, capturing Tobruk in June and forcing the British to retreat to Egypt. However, the second half of the year saw a reversal of German fortunes. British forces under General Bernard Montgomery gained the initiative in North Africa in the fall. At El Alamein, Egypt, in a battle that began on October 23, a huge Allied force, including new, highly-effective U.S.-built Sherman and Grant tanks, inflicted a massive defeat on the Axis forces. On November 2, Rommel was forced to order his army to retreat. The withdrawal eventually took Rommel all the way back to Tunisia. The Second Battle of Alamein was the first major Allied land victory of the war, and marked a turning point in the Desert War in North Africa.

On the Eastern Front, after continuing German advances in the first part of the year, Soviet forces counterattacked against the Germans at Stalingrad, encircling the German Sixth Army. By early December, German troops in the Stalingrad Pocket were starving and running short of ammunition and medicine. Hitler was facing his first major defeat of the war.

FALL OF BURMA

On January 12, Japanese forces moved northwest into Burma from Thailand. By mid-January, Japanese forces were in constant pursuit of retreating British forces. Crossing the Sittang River, Japanese forces moved toward Rangoon, the capital, which fell on March 7.

On April 10, the Japanese captured the oil fields at Yenangyaung. Chinese forces then entered Burma to bolster the faltering defense against the Japanese, but to little effect. The Japanese quickly advanced to encircle the Allies in the Mandalay area. On May 1, Mandalay fell to the Japanese and the Allies retreated again, heading for the Chinese province of Yunnan. Heavy rain hampered the Allied retreat.

A Japanese tank crosses an improvised bridge during the invasion of Burma in 1942.

FALL OF BURMA

Location	Burma
Date	January 12–May, 1942

Commanders and forces British: two British divisions, plus Chinese Fifth and Sixth Armies (Lieutenant General Thomas Hutton); Japanese: Fifteenth Army (Lieutenant General Iida)

Casualties British: 30,000; Japanese: 7,000; Chinese: 80,000

Key actions With the loss of Rangoon to the Japanese on March 7, the British Army in Burma was now isolated from its main base in India and dependent for its supplies on the stocks so carefully built up by General Hutton in the Mandalay area. Japanese air attacks between March 23–27 resulted in the withdrawal of all Allied aircraft from Burma to India. The rout of the Chinese Sixth Army by the Japanese between April 18–23 and the fall of Lashio on April 29 resulted in the Allies being forced to begin their retreat from Burma.

Key effects The Japanese had conquered 80 percent of Burma and had cut off the Chinese from their British and U.S. allies.

FALL OF SINGAPORE

Victorious Japanese soldiers celebrate their conquest of Singapore. The British had underestimated the power of the Japanese Army.

On February 8, two Japanese divisions, supported by artillery and air bombardment, landed on the northwest of Singapore Island, quickly followed by a third. Repairs to the Johor causeway then enabled tanks and 30,000 Japanese troops to advance, while, in the air, Japanese planes achieved supremacy. Confused orders often resulted in the Allied defenders making unnecessary withdrawals and much equipment was lost. Lieutenant General Arthur Percival, the Allied commander of Singapore, was forced to surrender to the Japanese on February 15, when the water supply for Singapore's residents and the 85,000-strong garrison was cut.

Japan had suffered fewer than 10,000 casualties in their campaign in Malaya. British and Commonwealth forces had lost a total of 138,000 men, and thousands more would die in captivity. The campaign was one of Britain's greatest defeats of World War II.

FALL OF SINGAPORE

Location	Singapore Island
Date	February 8–15, 1942

Commanders and forces British: Malay Command (Lieutenant General Arthur Percival), 138,000 troops; Japanese: part of Twenty-Fifth Army (Lieutenant General Tomoyuki Yamashita), 30,000 troops

Casualties British: 100,000, mostly prisoners; Japanese: 4,500

Key actions On February 8, the Japanese carried out successful landings on Singapore Island, and by February 11 they had captured most of the allied ammunition and fuel supplies, plus taken control of the main water supply. Also by this time, Japanese aircraft had seized total control of the airspace over Singapore.

Key effects The conquest of Singapore gave the Japanese a relatively safe passage from the Pacific into the Indian Ocean.

BATTLE OF THE JAVA SEA

BATTLE OF THE CORAL SEA

Under the command of Dutch Rear Admiral Karel Doorman, five cruisers and nine destroyers from four Allied nations engaged a Japanese force of four cruisers and 13 destroyers in the Java Sea on February 27. The Battle of the Java Sea lasted seven hours, due largely to the determination of Admiral Doorman to achieve a decisive result. He got one. His fleet was destroyed.

The long-range shooting from both sides was generally ineffective, despite the spotter aircraft that the Japanese were able to employ. Collectively, the Japanese heavy cruisers fired 1,619 8-inch shells, and made only five hits, four of which were duds. After the inconclusive opening engagement, however, the Japanese inflicted severe losses using their faster "Long Lance" torpedoes. Doorman was killed in the battle.

Japan deployed a large carrier force to surprise the U.S. Pacific Fleet in the Coral Sea in an attempt to establish control of the Solomon Islands. A key target was Port Moresby on Papua New Guinea, which would facilitate bomber attacks on Australia. The Japanese assembled a powerful force of aircraft carriers and other warships, but skilled U.S. codebreaking enabled Admiral Chester Nimitz, the U.S. Pacific Fleet commander, to prepare his forces. Nimitz deliberately withdrew from Tulagi in the Solomons before the attack, in order to reinforce the Japanese belief that only one U.S. carrier was operating in the area. On May 3, U.S. Rear Admiral Frank Fletcher's Task Force 17 damaged a Japanese destroyer, three minesweepers, and five aircraft off Tulagi during the Coral Sea engagement.

BATTLE OF THE JAVA SEA

Location   Java Sea, Pacific Ocean

Date   February 27, 1942

Commanders and forces   Allied: Eastern Striking Force, 14 warships (Rear Admiral Karel Doorman); Japanese: Eastern Invasion Force, 17 warships (Admiral Sokichi Takagi)

Casualties   Allied: 5 warships and 5 cruisers sunk; Japanese: 1 cruiser sunk and 6 destroyers damaged

Key actions   Admiral Doorman was killed and his flagship, *De Ruyter*, was sunk.

Key effects   The Allied defeat meant that no Allied warships remained in the Java Sea, which made the Japanese invasion of Java inevitable.

The Japanese Navy's forces gather for the battle against the U.S. Pacific Fleet in the Coral Sea.

BATTLE OF THE CORAL SEA

Location   Southwest of the Solomon Islands, Pacific Ocean

Date   May 7–8, 1942

Commanders and forces   U.S.: Task Force 17 (Rear Admiral Frank Jack Fletcher), Task Force 44 (Rear Admiral John Crace); Japanese: Carrier Striking Force (Vice Admiral Takeo Takagi), Port Moresby Invasion Group (Rear Admiral Tadaichi Hara)

Casualties   U.S.: 1 aircraft carrier destroyed, 1 damaged, 1 oiler and 1 destroyer sunk, 66 aircraft lost, and 543 men killed or wounded; Japanese: 1 small carrier destroyed, 1 carrier severely damaged, 1 destroyer and 3 small naval ships sunk, 77 carrier aircraft lost, and 1,074 men killed or wounded.

Key actions   On May 8, the U.S. carrier *Lexington* was scuttled after being seriously damaged. Also, the Japanese carrier *Shokaku* from the Carrier Striking Force was seriously damaged to the extent that it was removed from the battle and sent back to its base in Truk.

Key effects   This was the first naval battle in which the participating ships neither sighted each other nor exchanged naval gunfire. It was the first time in World War II that the Japanese experienced failure in a major operation. In addition, the U.S. victory prevented the Japanese seaborne invasion of Port Moresby. Finally, when the Japanese attacked the U.S. fleet at Midway the following month, the weakened Japanese were met by a stronger U.S. fleet than they had expected, and were defeated.

In late May 1942, General Erwin Rommel attacked the Allied-held Gazala Line in Libya while Italian armor also struck at Bir Hacheim. Although the British Eighth Army had 740 tanks, the Axis forces deployed their 570 tanks more effectively. However, Axis tanks suffered fuel shortages until the Italians penetrated the Gazala Line to bring up fresh supplies on the 31st.

By May 29, Axis forces had created a fortified area ("the Cauldron") inside Allied lines. Following the Free French withdrawal from Bir Hacheim on June 10–11, Axis armor then advanced east from the Cauldron to threaten the entire Eighth Army. British commander General Neil Ritchie ordered a withdrawal on the 13th.

The Japanese cruiser Mogami *after sustaining an attack by U.S. aircraft during the Battle of Midway.*

Japan's Admiral Chuichi Nagumo aimed to seize the U.S. base at Midway and then destroy the U.S. Pacific Fleet. Japan deployed a large fleet, including four large aircraft carriers, but U.S. codebreakers were able to warn the Pacific Fleet, which then converged to repel the Midway attack. Japan's I Carrier Striking Force was decimated by U.S. aircraft and three of its carriers were lost. Japan's aircraft carrier, *Hiryu*, then crippled the U.S. carrier *Yorktown* before itself being fatally hit. Japan's attempt to destroy the U.S. fleet by luring it into a surface battle had failed. As a result, Japan had lost half of its force of aircraft carriers.

BATTLE OF GAZALA

Location North Africa

Date May 28–June 13, 1942

Commanders and forces German: Panzer Army Afrika, 113,000 troops, 570 tanks and 500 aircraft (General Erwin Rommel); British: Eighth Army, 125,000 troops, 740 tanks, 700 aircraft (General Neil Ritchie)

Casualties German: 40,000, 114 tanks destroyed; British: 75,000 (including 33,000 taken prisoner at Tobruk), 540 tanks destroyed

Key actions On May 28–29, Axis forces got behind the British lines and created a fortress called "the Cauldron." The British did little to destroy this strongpoint. Then, on June 10, Rommel launched attacks from the Cauldron, and his tanks and antitank guns worked in close cooperation to knock out most of the British tanks. On June 13, facing defeat, General Ritchie ordered a British withdrawal.

Key effects The British retreated to Egypt, followed by Rommel's forces. This left the port of Tobruk isolated, and it fell to the Germans on June 21. Despite his victory, Rommel suffered from troop and equipment shortages because his vital supply convoys were being sunk by Allied aircraft in the Mediterranean. For their part, the British received reinforcements after the battle to rebuild their strength.

A German armored unit advances during Rommel's offensive against the British Eighth Army in Libya in 1942.

BATTLE OF MIDWAY

Location Pacific

Date June 4–7, 1942

Commanders and forces U.S.: Pacific Fleet, 3 carriers, 8 cruisers, 15 destroyers, 360 aircraft (Admiral Chester Nimitz); Japanese: Combined Fleet, 4 large aircraft carriers, 7 battleships, 11 cruisers, 41 destroyers, 272 aircraft (Admiral Chuichi Nagumo)

Casualties U.S.: 1 carrier and 1 destroyer sunk, 147 aircraft destroyed, 307 men killed; Japanese: 4 carriers and 1 cruiser sunk, 272 aircraft destroyed, 3,500 men killed

Key actions Before the battle, Nimitz had gained a priceless advantage when his Intelligence Service deciphered the Japanese radio code. This meant he knew about the Japanese plan for Midway and could react accordingly. On the morning of June 4, U.S. carrier aircraft sank three Japanese carriers (*Akagi*, *Kaga*, and *Soryu*) within a few minutes. The fourth Japanese carrier, *Hiryu*, was sunk later that day. Japan had lost her entire seaworthy aircraft carrier force. The Americans still had two left (*Yorktown* was sunk by Japanese aircraft in the Battle of Midway).

Key effects Midway was one of the most decisive battles of the war. Afterward, Japan was on the defensive and the United States grew ever stronger militarily. Japanese morale also suffered as a result of the defeat.

OPERATION BLUE

GUADALCANAL

On June 28, the Germans launched Operation Blue, which was intended to capture the Caucasian oil fields. Centered on the city of Baku on the Caspian Sea, the Caucasus region was the cradle of the Soviet oil industry. In 1940, 22 million tons (22.3 million tonnes) of oil were extracted, which was 72 percent of all the oil extracted in the USSR. In 1941, the figure rose to 23 million tons (23.3 million tonnes).

German forces made good initial progress, but on July 13 Adolf Hitler ordered simultaneous attacks on Stalingrad and the Caucasus, despite the strain this placed on his armies. Army Group B's advance toward Stalingrad was slowed after Hitler redeployed the Fourth Panzer Army to Army Group A's Caucasus drive. He believed that Army Group A would not be able to cross the Don River without reinforcements. Field Marshal Fedor von Bock, leading Army Group B, was later dismissed for opposing this move. The divergence of the two groups created a gap through which Soviet forces were able to escape.

At the beginning of August, Hitler then moved the Fourth Panzer Army back to Stalingrad to accelerate the German advance there. The Eleventh Army received similar orders. This, in turn, seriously strained the Caucasus advance.

OPERATION BLUE

Location   Caucasus, USSR

Date   June 28–August 19, 1942

Commanders and forces   German: Army Group South (Field Marshal Fedor von Bock): Sixth Army (330,000 troops and 300 tanks and assault guns); Second Army (95,000 troops); Seventeenth Army (150,000 troops and 180 tanks and assault guns); First Panzer Army (220,000 troops and 480 tanks and assault guns); Fourth Panzer Army (200,000 troops and 480 tanks), plus the Hungarian Second and Italian Eighth Armies. Luftwaffe: 2,690 aircraft; Soviet: Bryansk Front (169,000 troops), Southwestern Front (610,000 troops) and Southern Front (522,500 troops); tank total of 3,470

Casualties   Soviet: 250,000 killed or missing, 175,000 wounded; German: 40,000 killed.

Key actions   On July 13, Hitler decided to advance toward Stalingrad and the Caucasus at the same time. This reduced the strength of the forces attacking both objectives. In early August, he ordered the Fourth Panzer Army from the Caucasus back to the Stalingrad Front. This left Army Group A in the Caucasus thinly stretched in a massive area of land.

Key effects   The decision by Hitler to switch the Fourth Panzer Army from the attack on Stalingrad to the Caucasus on July 13 meant Stalingrad was not captured quickly. This allowed the Soviets to reinforce the city, which would have dire consequences for the Germans later in the year.

The U.S. 1st Marine Division landed on Guadalcanal Island to overwhelm the 2,200-strong Japanese garrison and capture the partly-built airfield. Tulagi was also taken. However, U.S. naval forces were subjected to air attacks and had to withdraw, leaving the Marines with supply shortages, but they were later relieved by air and sea. Japan sank four cruisers on August 9 and began landing forces by night to harass the Marines. U.S. forces defeated the first major Japanese attacks on the Tenaru River on the 9th. Fighting then centered on the airstrip known as Henderson Field.

By early December, the Japanese were establishing a well-defended front 6 miles (9km) west of Henderson Field. Japan had a 20,000-strong force, however, but the 58,000 U.S. troops were much better equipped and supplied on the island. Japanese prospects were poor.

On January 10, 1943, 50,000 U.S. troops launched a westward offensive to destroy strong Japanese jungle positions. A disease-ridden and starving force of 15,000 Japanese troops mounted fierce resistance and fought a rearguard action at Tassafaronga Point. The Japanese then decided to evacuate Guadalcanal.

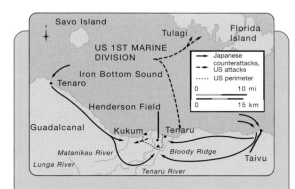

GUADALCANAL

Location   Guadalcanal Island, Solomon Islands

Date   August 7, 1942–February 9, 1943

Commanders and forces   U.S.: 1st Marine Division (General Alexander Vandegrift); Japanese: Seventeenth Army (General Haruyoshi Hyakutake)

Casualties   U.S.: 1,600 killed, 4,200 wounded; Japanese: 14,000 killed, 9,000 dead through disease, 1,000 taken prisoner

Key actions   The U.S. Marines defeated Japanese attacks against the Henderson Field air base between September 12 and 14, and again throughout October and November. The base was crucial to the U.S. plan to deny Japanese planes the means to attack Allied sea lanes.

Key effects   Victory on Guadalcanal Island was the United States' first land victory over the Japanese in the Pacific theater and paved the way for further victories in the Solomon Islands.

EASTERN SOLOMONS

BATTLE OF EL ALAMEIN

On August 23, 1942, a Japanese supply convoy, protected by the aircraft carriers *Ryujo*, *Zuizaku*, and *Shokaku*, attempted a resupply mission to Guadalcanal, but was intercepted by Vice Admiral Fletcher's Task Force 61, which also included three carriers (*Saratoga*, *Wasp*, and *Enterprise*). On the 24th, U.S. and Japanese carrier aircraft exchanged mutual blows, U.S. planes sinking the *Ryujo* and Japanese forces damaging the *Enterprise*. The carrier forces then separated, but the next day U.S. Marine dive-bombers flying from Henderson Field sank two Japanese transporters (*Jintsu* and *Kinryu Maru*) and the destroyer *Mutsuki*. Japanese supply runs to Guadalcanal were now to be made under more difficult night conditions.

General Bernard Montgomery's carefully-prepared attack by 195,000 Allied troops against 100,000 Axis troops at El Alamein in Egypt began with an enormous artillery bombardment on enemy positions, as well as numerous deception measures. Massive mine-clearance operations then enabled Allied armor formations to push forward and leave the infantry to widen the gaps. Field Marshal Erwin Rommel was in Germany, but immediately returned after the temporary commander of Axis forces, General Georg Stumme, died suddenly.

Severely lacking supplies, Rommel decided to withdraw from El Alamein. He delayed this for 48 hours, after Adolf Hitler's order to stand firm, but then ordered a retreat following further Allied attacks.

EASTERN SOLOMONS

Location   North of Santa Isabel, Solomon Islands

Date   August 24-25, 1942

Commanders and forces   U.S.: 2 aircraft carriers, 16 warships, 176 aircraft (Vice Admiral Frank J. Fletcher); Japanese: K Naval Force: 13 warships (Rear Admiral Raizo Tanaka), 3 aircraft carriers (Vice Admiral Chuichi Nagumo), 6 warships (Rear Admiral Hiroaki Abe), 6 warships (Vice Admiral Nobutake Kondo). Total Japanese aircraft: 170

Casualties   U.S.: 90 killed, 25 aircraft lost: Japanese: 1 aircraft carrier, 1 light cruiser, 1 destroyer, 1 troop ship, 90 aircraft lost

Key actions   On August 24, American aircraft sank the Japanese carrier *Ryujo* and Japanese aircraft badly damaged the U.S. carrier *Enterprise*.

Key effects   The loss of 90 aircraft, valuable pilots and an aircraft carrier was a severe blow to the Japanese Navy.

BATTLE OF EL ALAMEIN

Location   Egypt

Date   October 23-November 5, 1942

Commanders and forces   German: Panzer Army Afrika, 100,000 troops, 500 tanks (Field Marshal Erwin Rommel); British: Eighth Army, 195,000 troops, 1,000 tanks

Casualties   German: 59,000 killed, wounded and captured, 500 tanks destroyed; British: 13,000 killed and wounded, 432 tanks destroyed

Key actions   The British Operation Supercharge on the night of November 1/2 resulted in British armored divisions breaking through the last line of Axis defence. Thereafter, British tanks broke out into the open desert and the Axis forces began a long retreat westward.

Key effects   The Battle of El Alamein signaled the end of the Axis war effort in North Africa. The Suez Canal—a vital sea route for the Allies—had been saved, and the triumph over Rommel's Axis forces was the first British land victory over the Germans in World War II. Allied morale rose as that of the Axis nations dipped.

Gurkhas of the British Eighth Army go on the attack during the Battle of El Alamein in 1942.

BATTLE OF SANTA CRUZ

A Japanese bomber attacks U.S. warships during the Battle of Santa Cruz.

In October 1942, the Japanese Combined Fleet moved toward Guadalcanal in support of General Maruyama's offensive against the U.S. Marines on the island. U.S. Task Forces 16 and 17, containing the carriers USS *Hornet* and USS *Enterprise*, were sent to intercept the Japanese around Santa Cruz Island. A strike force of U.S. carrier aircraft missed their target on the 25th, and at first light on the 26th both the U.S. and Japanese put flights of attack aircraft into the sky.

Over the course of a four-hour battle, the Japanese carriers *Zuiho* and *Shokaku* were badly damaged, while USS *Enterprise* suffered a smashed flightdeck and USS *Hornet* was destroyed by two torpedo and six bomb strikes and had to be abandoned. The Japanese claimed victory in the battle, but had lost more than 100 pilots and aircraft, unacceptably high losses that rendered many of their carriers almost inoperable.

BATTLE OF SANTA CRUZ

Location Santa Cruz Island, Solomons, Pacific Ocean

Date October 26, 1942

Commanders and forces U.S.: Task Forces 16 & 17—two aircraft carriers, 21 warships, 136 aircraft (Rear Admirals Kinkaid and Murray); Japanese: four aircraft carriers, 39 warships, 11 submarines, 200 aircraft (Vice Admiral Nobutake Kondo)

Casualties U.S.: 1 carrier sunk, 1 destroyer sunk, 1 carrier heavily damaged, 2 destroyers heavily damaged, 81 aircraft destroyed, 266 killed; Japanese: 2 carriers heavily damaged, 1 cruiser heavily damaged, 100 aircraft destroyed, 500 killed

Key actions A coordinated Japanese dive-bombing and torpedo-plane attack left the carrier USS *Hornet* so severely damaged that it had to be abandoned. After losing this carrier, the U.S. ships retreated to the southeast. Kondo failed to pursue them.

Key effects U.S. losses of the carrier USS *Hornet* and also of a destroyer were more severe than those of the Japanese, who lost no ships in the engagement. However, after the battle, both sides were left with several badly damaged warships and the Japanese had lost another 100 aircraft and their irreplaceable pilots.

BATTLE OF THE BARENTS SEA

The Battle of the Barents Sea on December 30–31, 1942, saw the German pocket battleship *Lützow*, the heavy cruiser *Admiral Hipper*, and six German destroyers attempt to destroy an Allied Arctic convoy, codenamed JW-51B, which was on its way to Kola Inlet in the USSR. The convoy was carrying war materials to resupply Soviet forces, and the cargoes included tanks and vehicles, as well as a large quantity of aviation fuel. Although outnumbered, the Allied ships used superior tactics and exploited the German caution arising from orders not to sustain serious damage.

During the engagement, Germany had one of its destroyers sunk, while the Royal Navy also lost a destroyer and a minesweeper. The outcome of the battle outraged Adolf Hitler, who believed that the German fleet was tying down a massive amount of manpower and naval resources for very little result in terms of Allied merchant shipping sunk. Afterward, Hitler raged that the three German battleships—the *Tirpitz*, *Schleswig-Holstein* and *Schlesien*, the two pocket battleships the *Admiral Scheer* and *Lützow*, the battle-cruisers the *Scharnhorst* and *Gneisenau*, the heavy cruisers *Hipper* and *Prinz Eugen*, and the light cruisers *Emden*, *Köln*, *Leipzig*, and *Nürnberg*—would all be decommissioned and summarily scrapped. His idea was that, wherever possible, their guns would be converted for land use, but the German dictator's threat was never carried out

However, the Battle of the Barents Sea led to the end of significant sorties by major German surface vessels for the remainder of the war.

BATTLE OF THE BARENTS SEA

Location Barents Sea, north of North Cape, Norway

Date December 30–31, 1942

Commanders and forces German: 7 warships (Vice Admiral Oskar Kummetz); British: Force R, plus convoy escorts, 13 warships (Rear Admiral Robert L. Burnett)

Casualties German: 1 warship sunk, 330 men killed; British: 2 warships sunk, 250 men killed

Key actions · When Kummetz in the *Hipper* came under fire from three British ships, he ordered a ceasefire and a speedy withdrawal of all units. The German ships quickly retreated and the Allied convoy was saved.

Key effects Adolf Hitler was furious and ordered the German battle fleet to be scrapped, but this was later rescinded. However, henceforth, the German naval war effort would be carried out by German U-boats.

The opening weeks of 1943 saw the first major defeat for Hitler's armies. Encircled on the Eastern Front at Stalingrad in December 1942, the German Sixth Army was starving and cut off. In the first week of 1943, the Soviets gave German commander General Paulus two chances to surrender, but he refused.

On January 10, the Red Army launched a major assault around the perimeter of the Stalingrad Pocket. Within six days, German defensive positions were collapsing and soon the Germans were withdrawing into the center of the city. On January 23, the Soviets captured the last airfield in the pocket, ending German evacuation flights for their wounded. Paulus pleaded with Hitler to be allowed to open negotiations with the Soviets, but Hitler refused. Instead, on January 30, Hitler promoted Paulus to field marshal, as no German officer of that rank had ever surrendered. However, rather than commit suicide as Hitler expected, Paulus surrendered to the Red Army on January 31, and 93,000 German troops were taken prisoner, few of whom would ever see Germany again. Joseph Stalin had his first taste of victory over the Nazis, even though the city on the Volga named after him lay in smoking ruins and many, many thousands lay dead.

The Axis on the defensive

The German defeat at Stalingrad set the pattern for further Soviet gains on the Eastern Front during 1943, particularly the momentous victory at the Battle of Kursk in July, which saw Hitler's vaunted panzer force routed, and the Soviet Red Army advancing west on all fronts by the end of the year.

Meanwhile, battle continued to rage in the Atlantic, and one four-day period in March saw 27 merchant vessels sunk by German U-boats. However, thereafter, a combination of long-range bomber aircraft and the success of the Allied codebreakers based at Bletchley Park, England, began to inflict enormous losses on the Nazi U-boat fleet. Toward the end of May 1943, the commander of the German Navy, Admiral

Troops of the British Eighth Army pick their way carefully through the ruins of Catania, Sicily, in July 1943. Palermo, the capital of the Mediterranean island, fell at the end of that month.

Dönitz, withdrew the German U-boat fleet from the most heavily contested areas of the ocean. The Battle of the Atlantic was effectively over.

Elsewhere, in mid-May German and Italian forces in North Africa surrendered to the Allies, who used Tunisia as a springboard to invade the Mediterranean island of Sicily in July. By the end of that month, the Italian dictator Benito Mussolini had fallen from power. Mussolini was audaciously rescued by a German task force led by Otto Skorzeny, and established a fascist republic in the north of Italy. By mid-August, Allied forces had taken Sicily and, when Allied forces under General Montgomery crossed to mainland Italy at Calabria, it was the start of a long fight northward through Italy that was to prove slow and costly. On September 8, the Italians surrendered to the Allies, prompting a German invasion of northern Italy in a bid to take control of as much of the Italian mainland and to occupy as many coastal defenses as possible.

The Pacific campaign

In the Pacific, U.S. forces overcame the Japanese on Guadalcanal, and U.S. progress continued in the Aleutian Islands, New Guinea, and in the Solomon Islands. In November 1943, a U.S. force landed on Tarawa in the Gilbert Islands, to be faced with a network of bunkers protecting 5,000 determined Japanese defenders. More than 1,000 U.S. troops were killed before Tarawa was taken, in a taste of what the remainder of the Pacific campaign would be like for U.S. forces. British and Indian troops also began a guerrilla campaign against Japanese forces in Burma.

As the Soviet advance on the Eastern Front gathered pace, recapturing the cities of Kharkov and Kiev from German control, and Allied bombers began to attack German cities in daylight air raids, the leaders of the three main Allied nations met in Tehran, Iran, in November 1943. The top-secret conference saw British Prime Minister Winston Churchill, U.S. President Franklin D. Roosevelt, and the Soviet Union's Joseph Stalin give top priority to discussing detailed plans for Operation Overlord, the invasion of German-occupied Western Europe.

STALINGRAD

Operation Uranus, launched by the Red Army in November 1942, resulted in trapping the German Sixth Army, part of the Fourth Panzer Army, and what was left of the Romanian Fourth Army at Stalingrad. German commander General Friedrich Paulus then put his forces into a defensive posture as part of the grandly titled Fortress Stalingrad, and Luftwaffe chief Hermann Göering assured Hitler that his aircraft could resupply the "Stalingrad Pocket" by air. However, Wolfram von Richthofen, German commander of the 4th Air Fleet, believed it would be impossible to resupply the Sixth Army, as he had just 298 transport aircraft for the task of landing 350 tons (355 tonnes) of supplies a day (he needed at least 500 transports per day).

Therefore, German air operations to resupply their encircled forces at Stalingrad failed, and on January 10, 1943, the Soviet Don Front commenced Operation Ring, the destruction of the German Sixth Army in the Stalingrad Pocket. By this time, the German troops were freezing, starving, and severely weakened.

The Soviet offensive was brutally effective, as the Twenty-First, Twenty-Fourth, Fifty-Seventh, and Sixty-Fifth Armies, supported by the Sixteenth Air Army, launched a series of blistering attacks on the German positions. On January 30, Hitler promoted Paulus to the rank of field marshal, a move intended to prompt the commander at Stalingrad to commit suicide rather than surrender. Hitler reasoned that since no German field marshal had ever previously surrendered to the enemy, Paulus would not either. However, the next day Paulus surrendered his forces to the Soviets, and he was taken into captivity along with his weary troops. The momentous Battle of Stalingrad was finally over.

German forces were surrounded at Stalingrad and, after a fierce and desperate battle, German commander General Paulus was forced to surrender to the Soviet Red Army.

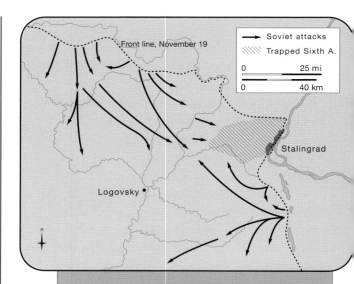

STALINGRAD

STALINGRAD

Location USSR

Date November, 1942–January, 1943

Commanders and forces German: Sixth Army, 300,000 troops, 2,000 tanks (General Friedrich Paulus): Soviet: Southwestern, Don, and Stalingrad Fronts, 1.1 million troops, 3,500 tanks (Marshal Georgi Zhukov)

Casualties German: 207,000 killed or wounded, 93,000 taken prisoner: Soviet: 480,000 killed and missing

Key actions The failure of the Luftwaffe to supply those German troops trapped in the Stalingrad Pocket due to bad weather and Soviet anti-aircraft defenses resulted in food and ammunition being in very short supply. The failure of a German relief attempt in December, Operation Winter Storm, doomed the Stalingrad garrison.

Key effects German forces in the south of the USSR were never again able to mount a large-scale offensive, so weakened had they been by the defeat at Stalingrad, which was a significant turning point in World War II. The Soviet Red Army, on the other hand, was able to launch an offensive along the whole of the Eastern Front that involved 4.5 million troops. This resulted in the Soviets regaining most of the territory they had lost to the German advance in 1942.

BATTLE OF KASSERINE PASS

BATTLE OF THE BISMARCK SEA

In Libya, North Africa, in January 1943, the British Eighth Army attacked Rommel's forces and pursued them to within 100 miles (160 km) of Tripoli. Although Rommel had been ordered to defend Tripoli, he decided to save his troops and abandoned the city on the 22nd to make a stand around Mareth. In February, Rommel launched an attack northwest from Mareth to attempt to break through Allied lines. In the Battle of Kasserine Pass, his forces struck the U.S. II Corps and caused panic among its ranks. German troops exploited poor U.S. command coordination and the inexperience of some troops. German attacks reached Thala before they lost momentum and Rommel ordered a withdrawal.

It was not until late February that Colonel General Jürgen von Arnim's Fifth Tank Army in northeast Tunisia finally launched a counterattack from the Mareth Line against the Allies. It was unsuccessful.

On March 20, Allied forces under General Bernard Montgomery launched a carefully-planned attack on the Mareth Line. The line's principal defenses along the banks of the Wadi Zigzaou were penetrated on the 21st–22nd, but the 15th Panzer Division successfully counterattacked. Montgomery, however, developed an outflanking move into a major offensive, and by the 26th the Axis forces had retreated north to the El Hamma Plain. The weakened German forces fell back to Wadi Akarit by the 28th, while many of their Italian allies surrendered. It was the beginning of the end of the Axis war effort in North Africa.

In early March 1943, a Japanese convoy heading for Lae, New Guinea, with 6,900 troops on board, was devastated by U.S. and Australian aircraft and by U.S. torpedo boats. The attacks began on March 2, and thereafter the Japanese ships suffered constant waves of attacks. By March 4, all the Japanese transports and four destroyers had been sunk, with 2,890 Japanese soldiers killed and only 800 finally making it to Lae.

A Japanese destroyer tries to escape bombs in the Bismarck Sea.

BATTLE OF KASSERINE PASS

Location Tunisia

Date February 19–25, 1943

Commanders and forces German: German Panzer Army Africa (Field Marshal Erwin Rommel), Fifth Panzer Army (General Hans-Jürgen von Arnim). Total German forces: 22,000 troops; U.S.: II Corps, 30,000 troops (Major General Lloyd Fredendall)

Casualties German: 2,000 killed and 34 tanks destroyed; U.S.: 5,200 killed and 183 tanks destroyed

Key actions U.S. tank units were scattered over the area in small groups, making them easy targets for German tanks and aircraft. The German attack was at first successful, but then U.S. forces counterattacked, supported by Allied aircraft. Arnim failed to make a supporting attack.

Key effects Kasserine was the last successful Axis offensive in North Africa. With the Americans advancing from the west and the British from the east, Axis forces were eventually trapped in a pocket around Tunis. In May 1943, they surrendered and 230,000 troops were taken prisoner.

BATTLE OF THE BISMARCK SEA

Location Bismarck Sea, in the vicinity of Lae, New Guinea

Date March 2–4, 1943

Commanders and forces U.S./Australian: Fifth Air Force (Lieutenant General George C. Kenney); Japanese: 8 destroyers, 8 transport ships, 6,900 troops

Casualties Allied: 2 bombers and 3 fighters shot down; Japanese: 2,890 killed, 8 transports and 4 destroyers sunk

Key actions Before the battle in the Bismarck Sea, Kenney had modified his A-20 and B-25 bomber aircraft, turning them into skip bombers. Besides carrying 500lb (227kg) bombs with delayed action fuses, these aircraft also had eight machine guns installed in the nose. Throughout the battle, the bombers made a series of devastating wave-level attacks against the Japanese ships.

Key effects The Japanese never again risked large convoys to reinforce their army on New Guinea. This gave General Douglas MacArthur, the Allied commander on the island, time to build up his forces for an assault against the Japanese base at Rabaul. For the remainder of the year, Kenney's aircraft went about establishing air superiority over the Japanese Air Force in the region.

OPERATION CARTWHEEL

BATTLE OF KURSK

With the northern coast of New Guinea mostly cleared of Japanese, General Douglas MacArthur launched Operation Cartwheel to isolate Rabaul. While his forces moved up from New Guinea, U.S. Marine units would take the largest of the Solomons, Bougainville. When the planned amphibious landings were complete, there would be a "ring" around Rabaul.

While U.S. and Australian troops landed on several small islands to build airfields, Kenney's Fifth Air Force and the U.S. Navy began hitting Rabaul through October and November. In the central Pacific, Admiral Chester Nimitz had begun his own offensive, and the Japanese Navy abandoned Rabaul to meet this new threat.

Meanwhile, U.S. troops invaded New Britain at Cape Gloucester and Arawe. The beaches at Arawe were undefended, but the landing at Cape Gloucester attracted a large Japanese air raid that sank one destroyer before Allied fighters intervened.

The next target was the vital airfield at Los Negros, northwest of New Britain. The 1st Cavalry Division, landing on 29 February 1944, ran into heavy opposition, but Los Negros was taken. The fall of Bougainville in late 1943 completed the ring around Rabaul, and Cartwheel ended. Although there were still 5,000 Japanese troops in Rabaul, they were left, suffering from disease and starvation, until the end of the war.

OPERATION CARTWHEEL

Location   Solomon Islands and New Guinea, Pacific

Date   June 1943-March, 1944

Forces and commanders   Allied: Allied Forces, Southwest Pacific Area (General Douglas MacArthur); Japanese: Eighth Army Area, 123,000 troops, 500 aircraft (General Hitoshi Imamaru), Southeastern Fleet (Admiral Junichi Kusaka)

Key actions   Operation Chronicle, June 30: no casualties. Operation Toenails, New Georgia, June 20-August 25: U.S. 5,000 killed and wounded; Japanese 1,671 killed. Operation Postern, September 4-15: Allied 300 killed and wounded; Japanese 350 killed. Operation Goodtime, October 25-November 12: Allied 62 killed; Japanese 205 killed. Operation Blissful, October 28-November 3; U.S. 13 killed; Japanese 143 killed. Other operations: Operation Cherry Blossom (the opening of the Bougainville campaign), November 1; Operation Dexterity, December 15, 1943-February 10, 1944.

Key effects   Operation Cartwheel became the model for Allied Pacific commanders throughout the rest of the war. The strategy was to advance quickly using air superiority and to bypass major Japanese strongpoints leaving them isolated and impotent It also involved attacking Japanese weak spots, avoiding frontal assaults wherever possible, and using techniques of deception and surprise.

The Germans believed that a victory on the Eastern Front would bolster morale at home and preserve the Axis coalition, while also demonstrating to the Allies that the Nazis could still achieve victory. From March to July 1943, the Germans gathered 900,000 troops in the Kursk area of the southern Soviet Union. However, the Red Army succeeded in establishing numerical superiority in troops and equipment in the region. Consequently, German units were exposed to aerial and land bombardment, while the Red Army prepared their elaborate defenses (including innumerable tank traps, obstacles, and antitank guns) to repel the expected German offensive at Kursk.

German Army Group Center's Ninth Army, south of Orel, and Field Marshal Erich von Manstein's Fourth Panzer Army, north of Kharkov, opened Operation Citadel with an offensive against the Soviet positions. The Ninth Army under Field Marshal Gunther von Kluge only penetrated 6 miles (9km) and lost 250,000 men.

German armored personnel carriers and assault guns rumble forward during the Battle of Kursk.

Increasing numbers of German troops reinforced the Kursk offensive, but the Red Army stood firm using a deep defensive network, while heavily-armed antitank units delivered concentrated fire against German armor. The Soviets quickly gained air superiority and their fighter planes provided valuable tactical support. These measures combined to prevent the German attacks penetrating the Soviet defenses.

Adolf Hitler called off Operation Citadel on July 13. The last major German offensive on the Eastern Front had been a costly failure. It was a huge disaster for Germany, not least because the Nazis' carefully-gathered strategic armored reserves had been wiped out in the fighting.

The Allied invasion of Sicily began in early July. The plan called for the British Eighth Army to advance up the east coast toward Catania and Messina. The U.S. Seventh Army was to protect the flank and rear. On July 23, the Seventh Army entered Palermo and then drove east toward Messina. In early August, U.S. forces were assisted by amphibious landings on Sicily's north coast. The Germans started withdrawing from Sicily on the 11th and evacuated 100,000 Axis troops before U.S. forces entered Messina on the 17th.

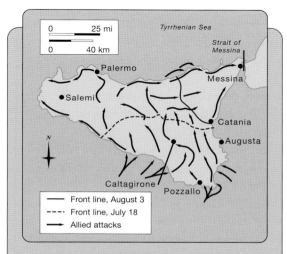

BATTLE OF KURSK

Location USSR

Date July 5-13, 1943

Forces and commanders German: Ninth Army, 335,000 troops, 590 tanks and 424 assault guns (Colonel-General Model); Fourth Panzer Army & Army Detachment Kempf, 350,000 troops, 1,269 tanks and 245 assault guns (Field Marshal von Manstein).

Forces and commanders Soviet: Western Front, 211,458 troops, 4,285 guns and mortars, 144 rocket launchers, 745 tanks and self-propelled guns, and 1,300 aircraft (Colonel General Sokolovsky); Bryansk Front, - 433,616 troops, 7,642 guns and mortars, 160 rocket launchers, 794 tanks and self-propelled guns, and 1,000 aircraft (Colonel General Popov); Central Front, 711,575 troops, 11,076 guns and mortars, 246 rocket launchers, 1,785 tanks and self-propelled guns, and 1,000 aircraft (General Rokossovsky); Voronezh Front, 625,591 troops, 8,718 guns and mortars, 272 rocket launchers, 1,704 tanks and self-propelled guns, and 900 aircraft (General Vatutin); Steppe Military District , 573,195 troops, 8,510 guns and mortars, 1,639 tanks and self-propelled guns (Colonel General Konev); Southwestern Front, 65,000 troops and 80 tanks (General Malinovsky)

Casualties German: 50,000 killed, 323 tanks destroyed; Soviet: 177,800 killed, 1,614 tanks destroyed

Key actions On July 12, a mass tank battle took place at Prokhorovka. Hundreds of tanks fired at each other at close range, but a counterattack by the Soviet Fifth Guards Tank Army stopped the German advance.

Key effects The German defeat at Kursk meant that the German armies on the Eastern Front were thereafter faced with a defensive war against an enemy that had more troops, tanks, and aircraft. Soon, the Red Army would be pushing the Germans back all along the Eastern Front.

INVASION OF SICILY

Location Sicily

Date July 9-August 17, 1943

Commanders and forces Axis: Italian VI Army, 300,000 Italian and 30,000 German troops (General Alfredo Guzzoni); Allied: U.S. Seventh Army (Lieutenant General George S. Patton), British Eighth Army (General Sir Bernard Montgomery). The Allied invasion force totalled 500,000 troops, airmen, and sailors

Casualties Axis: 29,000 killed and 140,000 taken prisoner: U.S.: 2,237 killed, 6,544 wounded; British: 12,843 killed and wounded

Key actions July 11 was the most dangerous day for the Allied invasion force. German aircraft and tanks attacked the U.S. Seventh Army's beachhead, but the tanks were driven off by naval gunfire and antitank guns. As darkness descended, the Americans still held, and in some areas had actually expanded, their narrow foothold on the island. By July 24, the Seventh Army had taken control of the entire western half of the island of Sicily, capturing 53,000 dispirited Italian soldiers and 400 vehicles, for the loss of 272 men.

Key effects Axis air and naval forces were driven from their island bastion and the Mediterranean sea lanes were opened to Allied shipping. Adolf Hitler had been forced to transfer German troops to Sicily and mainland Italy from other theaters of war, while the Italian dictator Benito Mussolini had been toppled from power, thereby opening the way for the eventual dissolution of the Rome-Berlin Axis and Italy's ultimate surrender to the Allies. The Allies quickly followed up their victory on Sicily by invading mainland Italy in September 1943.

A British mortar fires on German positions during the fighting north of Naples, Italy, in early October 1943.

German failure at Kursk meant that the Red Army could launch a series of massive offensives on the Eastern Front. On July 26, 1943, the German high command ordered forces around Orel to withdraw to the previously-prepared Hagen Line, just to the east of Bryansk. On August 2, Hitler ordered Field Marshal Erich von Manstein to hold the line firmly around Kharkov. However, German forces lacked the manpower, tanks, and artillery to halt the Red Army permanently.

When the Red Army advanced, the Germans were powerless. Between August 4 and 11, Red Army units retook Orel and Belgorod. The Voronezh and Steppe Fronts then neared Kharkov, which was retaken on the 22nd. The Soviets now threatened the southern area of the German front in Ukraine. On August 26, Soviet forces began an offensive to seize the eastern Ukraine and cross the Dniepr River, which formed a key part of the German defenses.

Further north, the Red Army recaptured Smolensk on September 25. Germany's Army Group Center was falling back in disarray. In Ukraine, the Red Army crossed the Dniepr. The Soviets recaptured Kiev on November 6. The German Seventeenth Army was trapped in the Crimea, as Adolf Hitler ordered the region must not be evacuated. Two bridgeheads—at Kiev and southwest of Kremenchug—had been created by the Red Army for their offensive to liberate the western Ukraine.

On September 9, 1943, Allied forces landed in the Gulf of Salerno. However, a German counterattack threatened the bridgehead. Only huge aerial and artillery support saved the Allied units. On September 22, British forces landed at Bari, seizing Foggia and its airfield five days later. British troops entered Naples on October 1. Elsewhere, the U.S. Fifth Army advanced northward, but halted on October 8 at the Volturno River, as the bridges had been destroyed by the Germans.

The British began their advance north across the Trigno River on the 22nd, but soon found that Field Marshal Albert Kesselring, the German commander-in-chief in Italy, had created a strong defensive system along the Garigliano and Sangro Rivers. It was known as the Gustav Line.

THE UKRAINE

Location USSR

Date July–November 1943

Commanders and forces German: 2.5 million troops (Adolf Hitler); Soviet: Red Army, 6 million troops (Joseph Stalin)

Casualties German: 213,000 killed and wounded; Soviet: 430,000 killed and wounded

Key actions July 12: Soviet Western, Bryansk, and Central Fronts defeated the German Second Panzer Army; August 3: Soviet Voronezh and Steppe Fronts defeated German Fourth Panzer Army and Army Detachment Kempf, retaking Kharkov on August 23; September 30: Soviet forces reached the River Dniepr, and then crossed it in November.

Key effects Vast areas of the central and southern Soviet Union were liberated by the Red Army. The German Army was being bled white on the Eastern Front, and ultimate defeat was now a distinct possibility. The Germans had lost thousands of tanks and vehicles, which meant that, as the Red Army became increasingly mechanized, the Germans had to rely more on horses for their transportation.

INVASION OF ITALY

Location Italy

Date September 9–December 31, 1943

Commanders and forces German: Supreme Commander South (Field Marshal Kesselring); Allied: British Eighth Army (General Bernard Montgomery), U.S. Fifth Army (Lieutenant General Mark Clark)

Casualties German: 15,000 killed and wounded; Allied: 21,000 killed and wounded

Key actions September 13: German forces nearly broke through to the U.S. landing beaches at Salerno. It took the Allies five days of desperate defending to repulse the Germans. In October and November, a skilful defense by Kesselring along the Garigliano and Sangro Rivers fought the Allies to a standstill. The British and Americans halted on November 15 to rest and regroup.

Key effects The Allies now had bases in southern Italy from which to launch strategic air attacks on the Balkans and on Germany; the Mediterranean was now secure; and German divisions were tied down in Italy opposing the Allied 15th Army Group and holding those areas in northern Italy, France, and the Balkans previously garrisoned by their former Italian allies.

GILBERT ISLANDS

The U.S. operation against Tarawa in the Gilbert Islands in November 1943 was among the bloodiest actions of the entire Pacific War. Tarawa Atoll was a little over 10 miles (16km) in length, but the bulk of Japanese defenses were concentrated on the islet of Betio, around 2 miles (3.2km) long and 0.5 miles (0.8km) wide.

The 4,500 Japanese troops on Betio, commanded by Rear Admiral Shibasaki, had created dense networks of fortified bunkers, trenches, and pillboxes, in which they sat out the U.S. Navy's preliminary bombardment of 3,000 tons (3,048 tonnes) of shells in only two-and-a-half hours. Bunkers constructed of sand-packed palm-tree logs proved especially durable.

The first wave of troops—from the U.S. 2nd Marine Division—went ashore at Betio on November 20, and walked straight into a hail of bullets and shells. Beach reconnaissance had been inaccurate, and many of the American "Amtrac" amphibious vehicles became grounded on a shallow reef, leaving the occupants to wade ashore under small-arms and artillery fire from the well-protected Japanese defenders. On the beach itself, the soft sand made it difficult for the U.S. soldiers to dig in. Radio communications between U.S. units

U.S. troops engage with the Japanese defenders on Tarawa. The battle was one of the toughest in the Pacific campaign.

broke down, resulting in 1,500 U.S. Marine casualties by the end of the day. However, a beachhead was finally established through sheer U.S. firepower, and over the next two days the Marines fought their way across Tarawa, the entrenched Japanese defenders contesting every inch of ground to the death.

A final suicidal charge by the Japanese on November 22 signified that resistance was crumbling, and on the 23rd the fighting finally stopped. The fanatical Japanese defense of Tarawa shocked U.S. leaders. For this tiny scrap of land, the Japanese high command had sacrificed nearly 5,000 of its men; astonishingly, only 17 Japanese soldiers surrendered, along with 129 Korean laborers.

GILBERT ISLANDS

Location Central Pacific

Date November 20–23, 1943

Commanders and forces U.S.: Task Force 54, 6 fleet carriers, 5 light carriers, 6 battleships, 6 cruisers, 21 destroyers plus support vessels, 900 aircraft, 27th Infantry Division and 2nd Marine Division, 18,000 troops (Rear Admiral Richmond K. Turner); Japanese: Betio, 4,800 (Rear Admiral Meichi Shibasaki); Makin: 800 troops (Lieutenant Seizo Ishikawa)

Casualties U.S.: 3,407 killed and wounded (Betio); 66 killed and 152 wounded (Makin); Japanese: 4,690 killed, 17 taken prisoner (Betio); 550 killed, 105 taken prisoner (Makin)

Key actions Betio: On November 20, the U.S. Marines went ashore on an abnormally low tide that stranded many of their landing craft on reefs hundreds of yards from the beach. Many had to wade ashore, exposing them to Japanese machine-gun fire. At the end of the day, 75 percent of the islet of Betio was still in Japanese hands. A Japanese counterattack would have driven most of the U.S. Marines back into the sea, but it did not materialize because the preliminary U.S. bombardment had destroyed Admiral Shibasaki's wire communications. Therefore, the Japanese commander had no way of mustering his men to take the offensive.

Key effects For the first time in military history, a seaborne assault was launched against a heavily-defended coral atoll, and it demonstrated the strengths and weaknesses of U.S. amphibious assaults. If the assault on Tarawa was not the overwhelming success that many later operations were, it had a greater long-term importance in that it paved the way for those operations. U.S. planners concluded that the preparatory bombing and shelling to be delivered on enemy-defended islands similar to Betio would have to be increased in both duration and weight, all of this with an eye toward the total destruction of accurately-located Japanese weapons and fortifications. The battle for Tarawa also highlighted the urgent necessity for timing naval gunfire and air bombardments to coincide with the initial movements of the landing craft taking the first waves of assault troops ashore. Another lesson learned at Tarawa was the need to have enough amphibious craft to carry ashore not only the first three assault waves but also the reserve waves to follow. On a strategic level, shorter U.S. supply lines to the Southwest Pacific could now be maintained and Japanese interference with them could be more readily neutralized. The victory on Tarawa meant that a base was gained for operations against the Marshall Islands.

With advances in Burma, New Guinea, and Guam, Japan began its last offensive in China, capturing further territory in the south to add to the acquisitions it had made in central and northern areas following the invasion of 1938. However, Japanese control was limited to the major cities and lines of communication, and fierce resistance often led by communist groups was widespread.

The Allied advance in Italy continued with beach landings at Anzio in January. The operation was not a great success, and it took until May for the invasion force to break out and link up with Allied units moving northward up the central spine of the peninsula. Until the Anzio breakout came, the Italian campaign was slow going for the Allies.

German forces in Italy had counterattacked Allied forces in February and the fighting saw the destruction of the medieval monastery at Monte Cassino after Allied bombing. Only at the end of May did the Germans retreat from Anzio. Rome, the capital of Italy, was finally liberated in June, on the day before the Allies launched Operation Overlord, the seaborne invasion of Normandy in northwestern France.

The D-Day invasion

On 6 June, 1944—D-Day—Overlord got under way as an armada of some 4,600 vessels landed more than 176,000 Allied forces on five Normandy beaches codenamed Utah, Omaha, Gold, Juno, and Sword. The landings were supported by almost 10,000 aircraft that ensured almost total air superiority for the Allies, bombing German defenses and providing cover for the troops being landed. The pessimistic predictions that had been made of massive Allied casualties were not borne out. On Utah beach, 23,000 troops were landed with just 197 casualties. Most of the U.S. casualties on D-Day occurred at Omaha beach, where the landing was significantly more difficult to achieve, meeting with fierce German resistance.

British Horsa gliders litter the fields northeast of Caen, France, on D-Day, June 6, 1944. Operation Overlord, the Allied invasion of Europe, had begun. The greatest invasion fleet in history had delivered a massive Allied force onto the beaches of Normandy, and World War II in Europe had entered its final phase.

Overall, however, the Allied landings in Normandy caught the Germans by surprise, and they were unable to counterattack with the necessary speed and strength. The reluctance of Adolf Hitler to reinforce his defensive positions in Normandy contributed to Allied success; the Führer was sure the Normandy landings were a mere diversionary tactic and that the real Allied invasion would come in the Calais region of France. By the time he realized his error, the Allies had secured their bridgehead and could not be dislodged.

Paris is liberated

Despite this, in the weeks following the landings, Allied progress was slowed considerably by the narrow lanes and thick hedgerows of the French countryside. Nevertheless, the port of Cherbourg was liberated by the end of June. Paris, the French capital, followed two months later. Hitler had ordered that Paris be destroyed before German forces could be evacuated, but the local Nazi commander disobeyed him, preserving the unique and historic city for future generations.

Hitler's troubles were compounded by a Soviet attack on the Eastern Front in June. This operation saw the Red Army drive 300 miles (450km) west to Warsaw, the capital of Poland, and resulted in 350,000 German casualties. By the end of August, the Soviets had taken Bucharest in Romania; Budapest in Hungary was under siege by the end of the year.

One glimmer of hope for Germany came in the Ardennes in France where, in December 1944, a German counteroffensive—known as "the Battle of the Bulge"—killed 19,000 Americans and delayed the Allies' march into Germany itself.

In the Pacific, by the start of 1944, U.S. forces had begun their advance toward the home islands of Japan. Their goal, however, remained thousands of miles away, protected by the vast expanses of the ocean. Adopting a strategy of "island-hopping," U.S. forces completed their conquest of the Marshall Islands in February. Further U.S. victories were to follow. The Battle of the Philippine Sea and those around the Mariana Islands further increased the pressure on Japan, whose use of "kamikaze" suicide pilots denoted their leader's increasingly desperate attempts to turn back the mighty U.S. naval forces.

MONTE CASSINO

On January 17, the Allies attempted to break through the Gustav Line. The British X Corps attacked across the Garigliano River and struck northwest toward the Aurunci Mountains and the Liri Valley. In response, the German commander, General Heinrich von Vietinghoff, moved up two armored divisions to counter the new threat. The pivotal point of the German defense was the town of Cassino and the monastery of Monte Cassino.

By January 24, the U.S. 34th Division established bridgeheads across the Rapido River to allow the armor to cross. In early February, Allied attacks edged closer to Monte Cassino before fierce German counterattacks stopped the advance. In mid-February, the U.S. 34th Division made a last attempt to capture the German-held monastery. Its attack was halted, however, and the unit was replaced by the 4th Indian and New Zealand Divisions of the British Eighth Army.

In mid-March Allied aircraft launched a massive raid against the unoccupied monastery of Monte Cassino. The New Zealand 2nd Division then launched an assault that took Peak 193. During the evening, the 4th Indian Division attacked and captured Peak 165. All Allied attacks on the 16th were frustrated, but on the 17th a breakthrough by the New Zealanders took Cassino railroad station. They failed, though, to complete the encirclement of the town. Despite further attacks by New Zealand troops under General Harold Alexander, the Germans, veterans of the 1st Parachute Division, remained in and around the monastery and repulsed all efforts to dislodge them.

On May 11, the Allied 15th Army Group began its offensive to outflank the monastery. On the 12th, the French Expeditionary Corps took Monte Faito, but the Polish 5th Division failed to capture Colle Sant'Angelo. On the 13th, the U.S. II Corps took Santa Maria Infante, and the British 4th Division began to enlarge its bridgehead across the Rapido River. On the 17th, the Germans evacuated the monastery at Monte Cassino, because the French Expeditionary Corps and the U.S. II Corps had broken through German lines. The next day, the Polish 12th Podolski Regiment stormed the ruins of Monte Cassino.

The ruins of the monastery at Monte Cassino, which was the scene of bitter fighting in 1944.

MONTE CASSINO

Location Italy

Date January 17–May 19, 1944

Commanders and forces German: Tenth Army (General Heinrich von Vietinghoff); U.S: Fifth Army (General Mark Clark); British: Eighth Army (Lieutenant General Oliver Leese)

Casualties German: 25,000 killed; Allied: 54,000 killed and wounded

Key actions After three battles at Cassino, in the fourth battle the Allies broke through the Gustav Line defenses and also broke through either side of Monte Cassino. On May 17, German commander-in-chief Field Marshal Kesselring ordered the entire Cassino Front be evacuated.

Key effects By May 25, with the Tenth Army in full retreat, VI Corps was driving eastward to cut it off. By the next day they would have been astride the line of retreat and the Tenth Army, with all Kesselring's reserves committed to it, would have been trapped. However, General Mark Clark ordered Truscott to change his line of attack from a northeasterly one to a northwesterly one directly toward Rome. The Germans escaped.

ANZIO

As part of the Allied attempt to break through the Gustav Line, U.S. troops made an amphibious landing at Anzio. Commanded by General John Lucas, the initial attack was almost unopposed and the road to Rome was open. Lucas, however, chose to dig in and missed the chance to strike inland. In mid-February, German forces attacked the beachhead, but Allied resistance forced the Germans to retire on the 19th.

A stalemate ensued, and it was not until May 23 that U.S. troops broke out from Anzio. Thereafter, steady gains were made, although the assault on the German defenses along the Adolf Hitler Line, from Terracina to Monte Cairo, caused heavy Allied losses.

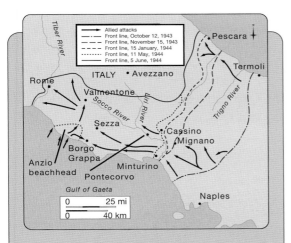

ANZIO

Location   West coast of Italy

Date   January 22–May 25, 1944

Commanders and forces   German: Fourteenth Army, 135,000 troops (General Eberhard von Mackensen); U.S.: VI Corps: 100,000 troops (Major General John P. Lucas), 2,000 aircraft; Task Force 81, 250 naval vessels; Task Force X-Ray, 74 vessels (Rear Admiral Frank J. Lowry); British: Task Force Peter, 52 vessels (Admiral Thomas H. Troubridge)

Casualties   Allied: 4,400 killed, 18,000 wounded, 6,800 taken prisoner; German: 5,500 killed, 17,500 wounded, 4,500 taken prisoner

Key actions   On January 22, Lucas made no attempt to drive inland from Anzio, despite there being no German forces in the area. This meant that Allied forces were quickly pinned down and contained within a small beachhead. Between February 28 and March 4, the Germans launched a series of heavy attacks against the Anzio beachhead, which were all repulsed with heavy German losses.

Key effects   The presence of a significant Allied military force behind the German main line of resistance, uncomfortably close to Rome, represented a constant threat. The Germans could not ignore Anzio and were forced into a response, thereby surrendering the initiative in Italy to the Allies. The 135,000 troops of the Fourteenth Army surrounding Anzio could not be moved elsewhere, nor could they be deployed to make the already formidable Gustav Line virtually impregnable.

OPERATION FLINTLOCK

On January 11, 1944, U.S. B-24 Liberator aircraft made a low-level attack on Japanese shipping around Kwajalein Atoll, sinking two vessels and damaging four others. The raid was just one of the many that took place around the Marshall Islands during January, as the U.S. prepared for a major land offensive there.

Operation Flintlock, the U.S. invasion of the Marshall Islands, began when a naval force set sail on January 22. Seven days later, U.S. carrier aircraft began a systematic one-week campaign against Japanese airpower and shipping around the Marshalls.

Operation Flintlock then continued with landings on Majuro Atoll and Kwajalein Atoll by U.S. Army and Marine Corps troops, supported by large numbers of land-based and carrier-based aircraft. Japan, at this time, was suffering unsustainable aviation losses in the Pacific theater, both of aircraft and pilots, and U.S. planners were coming to rely more and more on the ability of their forces to achieve air supremacy when plotting campaign strategy and tactics.

The Majuro landing proceeded smoothly, putting the U.S. troops ashore on an undefended island. In contrast, Japanese forces on Kwajalein Atoll resisted ferociously, and U.S. casualties were heavy. The U.S. declared the island secure by February 7.

At the beginning of February, the U.S. expanded its invasion of the Marshall Islands by landing Marines on Roi and Namur Islands. The two islands took two days to occupy.

OPERATION FLINTLOCK

Location   Marshall Islands, Pacific Ocean

Date   January 29–February 7, 1944

Commanders and forces   U.S.: Fifth Amphibious Force, 41,000 troops (Admiral Turner); Japanese: Marshall Islands Garrison, 28,000 troops (Admiral Masashi Kobayashi)

Casualties   U.S.: 3,000 killed and wounded; Japanese: 18,800 killed

Key actions   The U.S. invasion of Kwajalein Atoll on February 1 and Eniwetok Island on February 17.

Key effects   Rapid victory for U.S. forces in their campaign for the Marshall Islands added significant momentum to their Central Pacific drive and put Japanese positions in the Carolines and the Marianas within range of U.S. reconnaissance and bombing aircraft. In addition, new bases were acquired for the U.S. Navy. The Japanese Navy, intimidated by the approaching U.S. forces, reduced its fleet at Truk Island in the Carolines, formerly the bastion of Japanese air and naval power in the Central Pacific.

KOHIMA & IMPHAL

Waiting for the next Japanese attack: a British machine-gun position at Imphal, India, in late March 1944.

Operation U-Go, the Japanese offensive to drive the Allies back by destroying their bases at Imphal and Kohima in northeast India, began in early March. Japanese forces had orders to cut off the 17th Indian Division at Tiddim, while the 31st and 15th Divisions were to cross the Chindwin River farther north and attack Imphal and Kohima. On March 29, Japanese forces began the siege of Imphal, but by April 4 they had failed to destroy the Allied defense line. The British IV Corps could now turn its attention to the destruction of the Japanese. By April 13, the Japanese had been ejected from Nungshigum, and their 15th Division was being harried down the road to Ukhrul.

The Battle of Kohima ended with the remnants of the Japanese 31st Division withdrawing in good order. It had been their lack of supplies, rather than Allied attacks, which had forced them back.

KOHIMA & IMPHAL

Location India

Date March 6–June 22, 1944

Commanders and forces British: Fourteenth Army (Lieutenant General William Slim); Japanese: Fifteenth Army (Lieutenant General Renya Mutaguchi)

Casualties British: 17,500 killed and wounded; Japanese: 55,000 killed and wounded

Key actions By May 1, the Japanese had still failed to capture Kohima and Imphal. The Japanese divisions had not been receiving adequate supplies, including food, and the soldiers' health was rapidly becoming dangerously poor due to malnutrition. On May 31, Japanese troops withdrew from Kohima. On June 22, the battle at Milestone 109 was won by British and Indian troops, and the siege of Imphal was lifted.

Key effects In July, August, and September, the Japanese Fifteenth Army retreated south, pursued by the British. By the end of September, the Japanese force had almost ceased to exist.

D-DAY

On June 6, 1944, the Allies launched the greatest amphibious operation in history. D-Day, the Allied invasion of Normandy, codenamed Operation Overlord, began with the assault of Allied airborne forces, while seaborne forces landed on five beaches, codenamed Utah, Omaha, Gold, Juno, and Sword. The initial landings had mixed results: on Utah resistance was slight; on Omaha, the Germans pinned down Allied troops; on Gold and Juno, British and Canadians got off the beaches quickly: and from Sword, Allied troops were able to quickly link up with airborne units that had been dropped farther inland. By the end of D-Day, the Allies had a toehold in German-occupied Europe.

D-DAY

Location Normandy, France

Date June 6, 1944

Commanders and forces German: Army Group B—Seventh Army and Fifteenth Army (Field Marshal Erwin Rommel), Army Group G—First Army, Nineteenth Army (General Johannes von Blaskowitz), Air Fleet 3 (Field Marshal Hugo Sperrle). Total German strength: 850,000 troops, 1,552 tanks, 800 aircraft. Allied: British Second Army (General Sir Miles Dempsey), U.S. First Army (Lieutenant General Omar Bradley), plus British 6th and American 101st and 82nd Airborne divisions; naval forces (Admiral Sir Bertram Ramsay); air forces (Air Marshal Sir Trafford Leigh-Mallory). Total Allied strength: 176,000 troops, 4,000 ships and landing craft, 600 warships, 2,500 heavy bombers, 7,000 fighters

Casualties German: 9,000 killed and wounded; Allied: 3,000 killed and 7,000 wounded

Key actions First to land was the U.S. 4th Division on Utah Beach. It came ashore about 1,000 yards south of its intended landing place, avoiding heavy German defenses, and thus suffered few casualties. On Omaha, the first elements of the U.S. 29th Division and the 1st Division ran into stiff opposition and were quickly pinned down. On Gold, Juno, and Sword beaches, British and Canadian troops were supported by the specialized assault vehicles of 79th Armoured Division, which were able to break through the German defenses and establish a bridgehead.

Key effects By failing to defeat the massive Allied D-Day invasion force within the first 24 hours, the Germans had, in effect, lost the entire battle for Normandy. The war was entering its final phase.

THE MARIANAS

U.S. Task Force 58 began a heavy bombardment of Saipan, Tinian, Guam, Rota, and Pagan on June 11, prior to an assault on the islands, the occupation of which would allow the U.S. forces operating in the area to sever the lines of communication to Japan's units operating in the southern Pacific.

On June 15, landings were made on the west coast on Saipan by the U.S. 2nd and 4th Marine Divisions. The Japanese commander, General Yoshitsugu Saito, launched a mass charge against the U.S. 27th Infantry Division at Makunsho in early July. Despite losing hundreds of men to U.S. gunfire, the Japanese crashed through the U.S. lines. However, they soon lost their momentum and failed. Saito committed suicide and the island was declared secure on the 9th.

On July 19, U.S. battleships began a pre-invasion bombardment of Asan and Agat beaches on Guam, the most important island in the Marianas group. Two days later, troops of the 3rd Marine Division and 77th Infantry Division began landing on the island. A Japanese counterattack against the U.S. 3rd Marine Division on Guam on July 25 was defeated. Japanese resistance on Guam ended on August 10.

On the 24th, the U.S. 4th Marine Division landed on Tinian, and the island was declared secure after nine days of intense fighting.

U.S. troops use a howitzer to flush out Japanese defenders on the island of Tinian.

THE MARIANAS

Location Marianas Islands

Date June 15–August 10, 1944

Commanders and forces U.S.: Joint Expeditionary Force—110 transport vessels, 88 fire support ships (Vice Admiral Richard Kelly Turner), V Amphibious Corps—106,000 troops (Lieutenant General Holland M. Smith); Japanese: 57,500 (Lieutenant General Yoshitsugu Saito)

Casualties Saipan: U.S.: 14,111 killed and wounded; Japanese: 30,000 killed; Guam: U.S.: 7,800 killed and wounded; Japanese: 18,500 killed and taken prisoner; Tinian: U.S.: 1,899 killed and wounded; Japanese: 6,056 killed, 236 taken prisoner

Key actions On Saipan, the Japanese used many natural and manmade caves as defensive systems, with sophisticated camouflage and steel door protection. U.S. flamethrowing tanks proved to be the weapon that was effective against these caves. On Guam, on July 28, U.S. Marine and Army units moving from the north and south landing beaches linked up and took several of the hills that threatened the beaches, creating a consolidated line for the first time. On Tinian, the Japanese resorted to the same tactics they had used on Saipan, retreating during the day and attacking at night. However, tanks and artillery could be employed against them more successfully owing to the flatter terrain.

Key effects Victory in the Marianas brought U.S. Army and Navy forces close to their next major objectives in the Pacific: the Philippines and the Japanese home islands. American forces were now in a position to interdict directly Japan's vital East Indies oilfields, as well as to strike targets in the Philippines and Japan itself. On Tinian, for example, Ushi Point airfield and Gurguan Point airfield, enlarged and expanded, became vital bases, which, in the spring and summer of 1945, would unleash very long-range bombers against the Japanese homeland with devastating effect. Significantly, it was from Ushi Point airfield that the B-29 bomber *Enola Gay*, took off on August 6, 1945, to drop the first atomic bomb. It annihilated the Japanese city of Hiroshima.

On hearing of the U.S. assault on Saipan, a force of Japanese warships, under Admiral Jisaburo Ozawa, put to sea immediately. Ozawa's battle with the U.S. 5th Fleet, under Vice Admiral Marc Mitscher, began on June 19 but ended in disaster, when U.S. submarines sank the Japanese carriers *Taiho* and *Shokaku*. Defeat for the Japanese in the Battle of the Philippine Sea, later to be nicknamed the "Great Marianas Turkey Shoot," dealt a crippling blow to the Japanese naval air arm, not least through the loss of many combat pilots.

A Japanese ship under U.S. air attack during the Battle of the Philippine Sea, which virtually destroyed Japanese air strength.

BATTLE OF THE PHILIPPINE SEA

Location The Philippine Sea

Date June 19–20, 1944

Forces and commanders U.S.: Task Force 58–7 fleet carriers, 8 light carriers, 7 battleships, 8 heavy cruisers, 13 light cruisers, 69 destroyers, 891 aircraft (Vice Admiral Marc Mitscher); Japanese: Mobile Fleet–5 fleet carriers, 4 light carriers, 5 battleships, 11 heavy cruisers, 2 light cruisers, 28 destroyers, 970 aircraft (Vice Admiral Jisaburo Ozawa)

Casualties U.S.: 76 killed, 126 aircraft destroyed; Japanese: two fleet carriers sunk, 445 pilots killed, 476 aircraft destroyed

Key actions On June 11, more than 200 strike aircraft launched from Task Force 58's carriers attacked Japanese island airfields and destroyed 100 enemy aircraft. On June 19, four waves of Japanese aircraft were decimated by U.S. aircraft and antiaircraft gunfire, and 225 planes were destroyed. Also, two Japanese carriers were sunk by U.S. submarines. On the evening of June 20, 200 U.S. aircraft attacked the Japanese fleet, damaging two carriers and destroying 65 aircraft.

Key effects The Battle of the Philippine Sea was the greatest carrier aircraft battle in history, with the result that Japanese naval air power was all but destroyed. The loss of planes, and, even more so, the loss of experienced Japanese pilots, proved crucial in the battles that followed.

Operation Bagration was the Red Army's offensive against German Army Group Center in June 1944. The Red Army had a massive superiority in troops, tanks, artillery, and aircraft, and the Germans were unable to stop the offensive when it began on June 22. By June 28, the German Third Panzer Army had almost ceased to exist. On July 3, the Soviets captured Minsk, trapping 100,000 German troops. By July 21, the Soviet Second Tank Army was in Poland. When Bagration ended in August, Army Group Center had been wiped out.

OPERATION BAGRATION

Location Belorussia, USSR

Date June 22–August 29, 1944

Commanders and forces German: Army Group Center–580,000 troops, 9,500 artillery pieces, 900 tanks, 775 aircraft (Field Marshal Ernst Busch); Soviet: 1st Baltic Front–359,000 troops, 582 tanks and self-propelled guns, 1,094 aircraft (General Hovhannes Bagramyan), 3rd Belorussian Front–579,000 troops, 1,500 tanks and self-propelled guns, 1,991 aircraft (General Ivan Chernyakhovsky), 2nd Belorussian Front–319,000 troops, 251 tanks and self-propelled guns, 593 aircraft (General Georgiy Zakharov), 1st Belorussian Front–1,071,000 troops, 896 tanks and self-propelled guns, 2,033 aircraft (General Konstantin Rokossovsky). Total Red Army strength: 2.5 million troops, 5,200 tanks, 31,000 artillery pieces, 2,300 rocket launchers, 70,000 motor vehicles, 5,300 aircraft

Casualties German: 190,000 killed and wounded, 160,000 taken prisoner; Soviet: 178,000 dead, 587,000 wounded, 2,857 tanks and assault guns, 2,447 artillery pieces

Key actions On July 3, Soviet forces captured the city of Minsk, cutting off the German Fourth Army to the east. Five days later, the Fourth Army had been wiped out. On July 13, the Soviet 1st Ukrainian Front (840,000 troops, 14,000 artillery pieces, 1,600 tanks, 2,800 aircraft) launched the Lvov-Sandomierz Offensive against Army Group North Ukraine, which smashed through the German front in southern Russia.

Key effects Operation Bagration, combined with the Lvov-Sandomierz offensive in the Ukraine (launched on July 13), dramatically turned the tide of war against the Third Reich. The irreplaceable German losses in Belorussia, in conjunction with the Normandy landings and the July 20 attempt on Adolf Hitler's life, spread demoralization throughout the Wehrmacht's high command.

Operation Cobra, the Allied breakout from Normandy, began on July 25. After a massive aerial bombardment, U.S. VII Corps opened a breach in the German line between Marigny and St. Gilles, allowing Allied armor to get through. Within five days, the U.S. spearhead had reached Avranches.

THE LIBERATION OF FRANCE

Location France

Date July 25–August 25, 1944

Commanders and forces Allied: 12th Army Group (General Omar Bradley), 21st Army Group (General Bernard Montgomery)–1.5 million troops, 2,000 tanks; German: Commander-in-Chief West (Field Marshal von Kluge)–600,000 troops, 100 tanks

Casualties German: 500,00 killed, wounded and taken prisoner: Allied: 40,000 killed, 165,000 wounded

Key actions July 25–August 13: the U.S. First and Third Armies broke through German lines west of St. Lo in Normandy. Between August 13 and 19, 50,000 German troops were captured in the Falaise Pocket. The Allies then raced west and liberated the French capital, Paris, on August 25, as well as Brussels, the Belgian capital, in early September.

Key effects Although the German Army had suffered a massive defeat, it still retained good leadership and tight discipline. The war in the West would not end in 1944.

U.S. forces in Paris, France, after its liberation. The German commander of the city chose to ignore Hitler's order to destroy it.

By mid-August, Allied units had closed the Falaise Pocket, an area of encircled German troops. However, some 30,000 German troops escaped from the pocket across the Seine River. Canadian, British, and Polish forces coming from the north then linked up with the U.S. First Army driving from Argentan.

Paris, the French capital, was liberated on August 25, and six days later the U.S. Third Army spearheaded an advance toward the Meuse River as the British XXX Corps secured all the main bridges over the Somme River near Amiens. On September 1, the British Guards and 11th Armoured Divisions, both part of the British XXX Corps, reached Arras and Aubigny, and the Canadian II Corps, part of the Canadian First Army, liberated the French port of Dieppe. Two days later, the US First Army took Tournai and three German corps were crushed. The British Second Army also liberated Brussels, the capital city of Belgium.

British paratroopers in action near Arnhem in September 1944.

The Allied plan plan for a thrust across Holland to capture key bridges, Operation Market Garden, began on September 17. The British 1st Airborne Division landed near Arnhem, the U.S. 101st Airborne Division near Eindhoven, and the U.S. 82nd Airborne Division near Grave and Nijmegen, while the British XXX Corps advanced on the ground from the Dutch border. The 82nd and 101st took their bridges, but at Arnhem only one battalion managed to reach the bridge, where it was quickly cut off. XXX Corps reached U.S. troops at Eindhoven but failed to reach Arnhem. Realizing they had gone "a bridge too far," on the 25th, the Allies began evacuating the surviving British paratroopers.

ARNHEM

Location   Holland

Date   September 17-26, 1944

Commanders and forces   German: II SS Panzer Corps (General Willi Bittrich); Allied: 1st Airborne Corps, 35,000 troops (Lieutenant General Lewis Brereton) (U.S. 82d Airborne Division & 101st Airborne Division, British 1st Airborne Division, Polish 1st Parachute Brigade), British XXX Corps (Lieutenant General Horrocks)

Casualties   German: 10,000 killed and wounded; Allied: 17,200 killed, wounded, and taken prisoner

Key actions   Because there were not enough transport aircraft and gliders, it would take 2 or 3 days to move all the Allied troops and their equipment to their destinations. This reduced the element of surprise. On September 17, at Arnhem, the British paratroopers failed to capture and hold the bridge because of German resistance. On the same day, XXX Corps only reached Valkenswaard, not their intended target, Eindhoven. Operation Market Garden was already behind schedule. On September 21, the British troops at the bridge at Arnhem were overwhelmed. The survivors formed a pocket on the northern bank of the Neder Rijn. Two days later XXX Corps was driven back.

Key effects   The German defense in the West was still intact. The war would not end in 1944, and the Allies would still have to cross the Rhine River to enter the German homeland.

Following the U.S. landings on Leyte, the Japanese put in motion their Sho Plan, in which a part of the Combined Fleet was used to decoy the U.S. carrier force, while the remainder were concentrated against the U.S. landing area and attempted to destroy the American amphibious armada.

The resulting naval battle of Leyte Gulf had four distinct phases: the Battle of the Sibuyan Sea; the Battle of the Surigao Strait; the Battle of Samar; and the Battle of Cape Engano. The final result of these encounters was that the Japanese Combined Fleet was finished as a fighting force, not least because its losses in trained pilots were irreplaceable. Furthermore, the Battle of Leyte Gulf marked the undeniable collapse of Japanese naval power in the Pacific theater. From that point onward, the Japanese suicide air attacks that had had their inauguration over Leyte Gulf became a regular feature of an increasingly desperate Japanese defense that, in reality, could no longer offer any effective opposition to the mighty U.S. Navy.

BATTLE OF LEYTE GULF

Location   Leyte Gulf, The Philippines

Date   October 23-26, 1944

Forces and commanders   U.S.: Third Fleet (Admiral "Bull" Halsey), Seventh Fleet (Vice Admiral Kinkaid). Total U.S. strength: 1,500 aircraft, 32 aircraft carriers, 12 battleships, 23 cruisers. Japanese: Northern Force (Admiral Ozawa), Southern Force (Vice Admiral Nishimura), Center Force (Vice Admiral Kurita), Second Striking Force (Vice Admiral Shima). Total Japanese strength: 130 aircraft, 4 aircraft carriers, 2 hybrid aircraft carriers, 7 battleships, 19 cruisers, 33 destroyers

Casualties   U.S.: 10 ships sunk; Japanese: 35 ships sunk

Key actions   October 24: The Battle of the Sibuyan Sea. U.S. aircraft launched massive attacks on the ships of the Southern Force and Center Force. They immediately hit the battleships *Yamato* and *Musashi*, and the heavy cruiser *Myoko*, which was forced to head back to Brunei. *Musashi* was eventually sunk. The Center Force was forced to retreat west. October 24-25: The Battle of Surigao Strait. The Japanese Southern Force was engaged by ships of the Seventh Fleet. Two Japanese battleships, one cruiser, and three destroyers were sunk by U.S. naval gunfire. The Japanese Second Striking Force, following on behind, retreated west. October 25-26: Battle off Cape Engaño. Aircraft of the U.S Third Fleet engaged the aircraft carriers of the Northern Force. Ozawa lost all four of his carriers, one of his three cruisers, and two of his nine destroyers, and all of his 130 aircraft. October 25: Battle off Samar. The Japanese Center Force fought the ships of the Seventh Fleet and sank four U.S. ships. However, Kurita lost three of his own ships, broke off the battle and then headed north

Key effects   The Americans had eliminated the threat that Japanese warships had posed to amphibious operations in the Philippines and had effectively isolated the Japanese garrisons on the islands for the duration of the war.

THE ARDENNES OFFENSIVE (BATTLE OF THE BULGE)

Hitler launched the Ardennes Offensive on December 16. It was his attempt to capture Antwerp, Belgium, thereby splitting the Allies in northern Europe in two. Surprise was total, and dense cloud and fog negated Allied air superiority, but the Germans failed to take the towns of St. Vith and Bastogne quickly, as planned. By the 22nd, the Americans, having suffered heavy casualties at St. Vith, pulled back from the town, but the 10th, 28th, and 101st Airborne Divisions held out stubbornly in Bastogne against one infantry and two panzer divisions. On the same day, the Germans mounted their last attempt to reach the Meuse River.

On December 26, U.S. forces counterattacked against the north and south of the German "bulge" into the Ardennes, and Bastogne was relieved. At Bastogne at the end of December, General George Patton's forces attacked northeast toward Houffalize. At the same time, General Hasso von Manteuffel, commander of the German Fifth Panzer Army, launched another attempt to cut the corridor into Bastogne and take the town. The fighting was intense, but Patton's forces stood firm and defeated the German attack.

The last German attack was defeated in early January 1945, and the Allied counterattack began: on the northern flank the U.S. First Army attacked the northern sector of the bulge, while the southern sector was assaulted by the U.S. Third Army. In the bulge itself, Hitler ordered a German withdrawal to Houffalize on the 8th. However, in the face of Allied superiority in men and hardware, the Germans were forced to retreat farther east, and the U.S. First and Third Armies linked up at Houffalize on the 16th.

Aided by secrecy and poor weather conditions, the initial assaults of the German Ardennes offensive met with success.

THE ARDENNES OFFENSIVE

Location   Ardennes region, Belgium

Date   December 16, 1944–January 16, 1945

Forces and commanders   German: Army Group B–Sixth Panzer Army, Fifth Panzer Army, Seventh Army, Fifteenth Army (Field Marshal Model); German strength (on December 16): 200,000 troops, 1,900 artillery pieces, 1,800 tanks. U.S.: First Army (Lieutenant General Courtney Hodges), Third Army (Lieutenant General George S. Patton). U.S. strength (on December 16): 83,000 troops, 242 tanks, 182 tank destroyers, 394 artillery pieces

Casualties   German: 100,000 killed, wounded, and taken prisoner; U.S.: 81,000 killed, wounded, and taken prisoner

Key actions   The German planned to have their panzers at the Meuse River four days after the attack began. The stubborn American defense at Bastogne and St. Vith made this impossible. On January 1, 1945, more than 1,000 German aircraft attacked Allied airfields in Holland and Belgium. They destroyed roughly 300 Allied aircraft, but their loss of more than 230 pilots was a major blow to the Luftwaffe, whose lack of trained aviators was critical.

Key effects   Massive German losses in manpower, equipment, supplies, and morale during the "Battle of the Bulge," as the German Ardennes offensive became known, were instrumental in bringing about a more rapid end to the war in Europe.

The **New Year** saw the Soviet liberation of the Nazi death camp at Auschwitz in Poland, and the revelation of the Holocaust—the systematic plan to annihilate the Jewish population of Europe. Its scale became ever clearer as more death camps were liberated in the months that followed. It is estimated that, during World War II, some 6 million Jews, along with numerous others, were killed by the Nazis in an operation they had euphemistically labeled "The Final Solution."

While the bombing campaigns of the Blitz were over, German V1 and V2 rockets continued to drop on London. In return, a massive Allied bombing raid on Dresden, on the Elbe River, devastated the German city in a huge firestorm. Estimates of the death toll caused by the raid on the night of February 13–14 range from 40,000 to 100,000 people.

The fall of Nazi Germany

In the ground war in Europe, the Soviet Red Army continued its offensive into the German homeland from the east, while, from the west, Allied forces secured a bridge across the Rhine River at Remagen in March, and troops began to pour into Germany. The race for Berlin, the German capital, was on. The Soviet Red Army won, reaching Berlin on April 21, where bitter street-by-street fighting ensued between Soviet troops and the remnants of German resistance, including many fanatical members of the Hitler Youth.

As the Red Army closed in, Adolf Hitler, deep in his bunker beneath Berlin, killed himself on April 30, two days after the Italian fascist leader Benito Mussolini had been captured and hanged by Italian partisans. Germany surrendered unconditionally on May 7, and the next day was celebrated by the Allies as "VE-Day" (Victory in Europe Day). The war in Europe was over.

In the Pacific, however, war continued to rage. The British advanced further into Burma and, in February, the Americans invaded Iwo Jima, one of the heavily-defended Japanese-held islands that formed a ring protecting Japan itself. The fighting on Iwo Jima was intense, as U.S. forces battled against 21,000 Japanese

U.S. troops and vehicles in Bastogne, Belgium. Although cut off from the main Allied armies, the U.S. force resisted German attacks during the Battle of the Bulge, until rescued in January 1945.

defenders. After an aerial bombardment on Japanese positions that lasted for 72 days, U.S. troops landed on Iwo Jima on February 19, 1945, but could not declare the island secure until March 26. The 36 days of bitter fighting took a terrible toll on both sides, U.S. forces suffering almost 6,000 dead and more than 17,000 wounded. Only a tiny fraction of the Japanese force survived. Similar resistance was put up by the Japanese in the Philippines and on the island of Okinawa, but, again, U.S. forces prevailed. The fighting was of such intensity because the Japanese were willing to die almost to a man to protect their homeland, as the might of U.S. Pacific forces bore down on Japan itself.

Dropping atomic bombs on Japan

Even as these battles were still being fought, U.S. commanders were formulating plans for the invasion of Japan. However, fears of fierce resistance and huge casualties prompted Harry S. Truman (the new U.S. president) to sanction the use of atomic bombs against Japan. Such weapons had been in development since 1942, and on August 6 one of them, codenamed *Little Boy*, was dropped onto the Japanese city of Hiroshima, home to a population of 245,000. In an instant, 60 percent of the city was destroyed, with around 66,000 people killed and 70,000 wounded. A U.S. ultimatum to Japan's High Command to surrender unconditionally was ignored, and so, three days later, another atomic bomb, codenamed *Fat Man*, was dropped on the city of Nagasaki. An estimated 40,000 people were killed and 25,000 wounded. No country could withstand such devastating attacks, and the Japanese government, led by Emperor Hirohito, finally convinced the Japanese military that to continue the fight would be futile. Japan surrendered to the Americans on August 15, 1945. World War II had finally come to an end.

The biggest conflict in human history had lasted almost six years. Some 50 million people had been killed. Of those, 15 million were soldiers, 20 million were Soviet civilians, and 6 million were Jews. After witnessing the Japanese sign the formal document of surrender on September 2, 1945, General Douglas MacArthur said: "Let us pray that peace be now restored to the world and God will preserve it always."

On January 9, preceded by a heavy bombardment, units of the U.S. Sixth Army, commanded by Lieutenant General Walter Krueger, made unopposed amphibious landings on Luzon in the Philippines. Japanese resistance was light, and by February 3 the U.S. XIV Corps was beginning its attack against Manila, which was defended by 17,000 Japanese troops under Rear Admiral Sanji Iwabuchi. The garrison, after destroying the city (the "Rape of Manila"), was wiped out.

U.S. forces began to clear the Japanese from the entrance to Manila Bay, Luzon. The peninsula of Bataan fell relatively easily, though Corregidor proved a harder nut to crack. The assault began on February 16 with a battalion of U.S. paratroopers dropping on the southwest heights of the island. Simultaneously, an amphibious assault by a battalion of infantry took place on the southern shore. By the evening of the

Following their unopposed landing, troops of the U.S. Sixth Army examine a knocked-out Japanese tank on Luzon.

26th, almost the whole of the island was in U.S. hands. The Japanese garrison refused to surrender, and was virtually wiped out in the fighting.

Thereafter, U.S. forces cleared the islands one by one: a regiment of the U.S. 41st Division captured the island of Palawan on February 28. On March 18, the U.S. 40th Division landed on Panay, secured it, and then moved on to clear nearby Guimaras Island. It took U.S. forces four months to secure the island of Mindanao, which finally fell on July 26.

BATTLE FOR LUZON

Location Luzon, the Philippines

Date January 9–August 15, 1945

Commanders and forces U.S.: Sixth Army (General Krueger), Eighth Army (General Eicheberger); Japanese: Fourteenth Army, 250,000 troops (General Yamashita)

Casualties U.S.: 7,933 killed, 32,732 wounded; Japanese: 192,000 killed, 9,700 taken prisoner

Key actions January 9: U.S. forces made a virtually unopposed landing on Luzon. Between February 3 and March 4, U.S. troops captured Manila after fierce fighting in which 16,600 Japanese troops were killed. Also U.S. forces had captured the fortress of Corregidor by February 27.

Key effects General Douglas MacArthur had fulfilled the promise he had made two years before ("I will return") when he was forced to leave the Philippines when the Japanese invaded.

THE VISTULA-ODER OFFENSIVE

German rockets scream through the air as the Second Army tries to halt the Soviet 2nd Belorussian Front in Poland.

The Red Army's Vistula-Oder offensive, which began on January 12, 1945, made excellent progress, and by the 17th, Zhukov's Second Guards Tank Army had reached Sochaczew. By January 19, after heavy fighting, the 1st Ukrainian Front liberated Cracow, the former capital of Poland. The German Third and Fourth Panzer Armies were now isolated in East Prussia, and the German front was falling apart. By the end of January, the left wing of the 1st Ukrainian Front had reached the Oder River, where some of its leading units set up a bridgehead. This ended one of the greatest strategic operations of the whole war.

The Red Army had advanced 355 miles (568 km), liberated the whole of Poland and a large part of Czechoslovakia, reached the Oder River on a broad front, and now lay only 37.5 miles (60 km) from the heart of the Third Reich—Berlin itself.

THE VISTULA-ODER OFFENSIVE

Location   German and Poland

Date   January 12-February 3, 1945

Commanders and forces   German: Army Group Center–Third Panzer Army, Fourth Army, Second Army (Colonel General Hans Reinhardt), Army Group A–Ninth Army, Fourth Panzer Army, Seventeenth Army, First Panzer Army (Colonel General Josef Harpe); Soviet: 3rd Belorussian Front (Colonel General Cherniakovsky), 2d Belorussian Front (Marshal Rokossovsky), 1st Belorussian Front (Marshal Zhukov), 1st Ukrainian Front (Marshal Konev), 4th Ukrainian Front (Colonel General Petrov). Total: 4 million troops

Casualties   German: 500,000 killed and taken prisoner; Soviet: 43,000 killed, 149,000 wounded

Key actions   The Soviet offensive was so powerful all along the front that by January 31, 1945, Red Army tanks had reached the Oder River, 250 miles (400 km) from their starting positions just two weeks earlier.

Key effects   At the end of the offensive, the Red Army was only 37.5 miles (60 km) from the German capital, Berlin. The Soviets would now amass more than two million troops for their attack on the city.

IWO JIMA

The island of Iwo Jima was vital to U.S. plans for attacking mainland Japan, as the island had two air bases and was only three hours' flying time from Tokyo. Under General Holland M. Smith, the U.S. 3rd, 4th, and 5th Marine Divisions landed on February 19. Resistance was at first light, but then the attackers were hit by intense fire from the Japanese garrison. However, despite heavy casualties, within days the U.S. Marines had raised the U.S. flag on the summit of Mount Suribachi. The island was finally declared secure by the Americans following a prolonged battle.

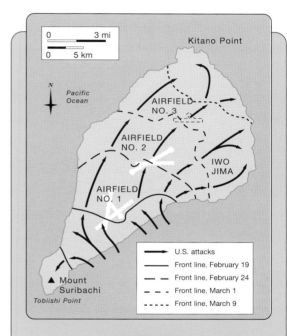

IWO JIMA

Location   Iwo Jima, Pacific

Date   February 19-March 26, 1945

Forces and commanders   U.S.: Fifth Amphibious Corps–3rd Marine Division, 4th Marine Division, 5th Marine Division–70,000 troops (General Holland M. Smith), U.S. Navy Fifth Fleet–485 surface ships (Admiral Raymond A. Spruance); Japanese: 23,000 troops (Lieutenant General Tadamichi Kuribayashi)

Casualties   U.S.: 6,821 killed, 19,217 wounded; Japanese: 20,867 killed, 1,083 taken prisoner

Key actions   Mount Suribachi in the south fell to the U.S. Marines on February 23. Five days later, they had captured two-thirds of the island. On March 5, the troops of the U.S. 5th Marine Division defeated a large-scale Japanese counterattack.

Key effects   The capture of Iwo Jima breached the Japanese inner defensive ring around their homeland. To keep up the momentum, the Americans next planned to move even closer to the Japanese home islands to capture Okinawa, only 360 miles (576 km) from Japan.

Okinawa, only 325 miles (520 km) from Japan, had two airfields on the western side and two sheltered bays on the east coast, making it an excellent springboard for the proposed invasion of the Japanese mainland. Admiral Chester W. Nimitz, commander-in-chief U.S. Pacific Fleet and Pacific Ocean areas, had assigned Vice Admiral Richmond Turner as commander of the amphibious forces and Vice Admiral Marc Mitscher as commander of the fast carrier forces. The U.S. Tenth Army was led by Lieutenant General Simon B. Buckner. The U.S. invasion of the island was codenamed Operation Iceberg. The amphibious landing by the U.S. II Amphibious Corps and XXIV Corps was virtually unopposed. The Japanese commander, Major General Mitsuru Ushijima, had withdrawn his forces behind Shuri, where he had built a major defensive line.

After a momentous battle, Japanese resistance ended on June 29. Ushijima, realizing that the situation was hopeless, committed ritual suicide in a cave near Mabuni. The battle, which had seen the extensive use of Japanese kamikaze attacks, claimed the lives of more than 130,000 Japanese military personnel.

Within two days of the Red Army launching its Berlin Offensive, the German Ninth Army had been shattered. By April 21, Soviet forces were fighting in the city. On April 28, Soviet troops were just 1 mile (1.6km) from Hitler's bunker below the Chancellery. The next day, around the Reichstag, the German LVI Panzer Corps was almost out of ammunition. Hitler ordered the troops to fight to the last man and bullet.

On April 30, Soviet troops engaged SS soldiers in a vicious room-by-room fight for the Reichstag. Hitler committed suicide the same day. On May 1, General Krebs, chief of the General Staff, asked the Soviets for surrender terms, but Stalin wanted unconditional surrender and so the fighting went on. The next day General Weidling, commander of the Berlin garrison, surrendered the city to the Soviet Red Army.

OKINAWA

Location   Ryukyu Island chain

Date   April 1–June 29, 1945

Forces and commanders   U.S.: Fifth Fleet—1,300 ships (Admiral Raymond A. Spruance), Tenth Army—183,000 troops (Lieutenant General Simon Bolivar Buckner); Japanese: Thirty-Second Army—150,000 troops (General Ushijima)

Casualties   U.S.: 12,000 killed, 36,000 wounded, 763 aircraft destroyed, 36 ships sunk, 368 ships damaged. Japanese: 107,539 soldiers killed and 23,764 sealed in caves or buried, 10,755 taken prisoner, 42,000 civilians killed, 7,830 aircraft destroyed, and 16 warships sunk

Key actions   The battle for the island was split into four phases: first, the advance to the eastern coast (April 1–4); second, the clearing of the northern part of the island (April 5–18); third, the occupation of the outlying islands (April 10–June 26); and fourth, the main battle against the dug-in elements of the Japanese 32nd Army, which began on April 6 and did not end until June 21. On April 7, the Japanese battleship *Yamato* was sunk on its way to Okinawa by U.S. aircraft. Ushijima committed suicide on June 16.

Key effects   The military value of Okinawa to U.S. forces was great. The island was sufficiently large to house great numbers of troops; it provided numerous airfield sites close to the enemy's homeland; and it furnished fleet anchorage, which would help the U.S. Navy to keep its operations active. However, the scale of losses suffered on Iwo Jima and Okinawa convinced the U.S. president and his military chiefs that an invasion of Japan would result in unacceptably high losses. The decision was then taken to use atomic bombs on Japan to hasten the end of the war.

BATTLE OF BERLIN

Location   Germany

Date   April 16–May 2, 1945

Forces and commanders   German: Army Group Vistula—Third Panzer and Ninth Armies, with LVI Panzer Corps in reserve—200,000 troops, 750 tanks and assault guns, 1,500 artillery pieces (Generaloberst Gotthard Heinrici); Army Group Center—Fourth Panzer Army—100,000 troops and 200 tanks and assault guns (Field Marshal Ferdinand Schörner); Soviet: 1st Belorussian Front (Marshal Georgi Zhukov), 2d Belorussian Front (Marshal Konstantin Rokossovsky), 1st Ukrainian Front (Marshal Ivan Konev). Total Soviet strength: 2.5 million troops, 41,000 artillery pieces, 6,200 tanks and assault guns, 100,000 motor vehicles, 7,200 aircraft

Casualties   German: 500,000 killed and taken prisoner; Soviet: 81,000 killed, 272,000 wounded

Key actions   April 21: the artillery of the 1st Belorussian Front began shelling Berlin's eastern suburbs. The next day, Soviet troops broke into the city's northeastern and eastern suburbs. On April 28, Soviet troops were only 1 mile (1.6 km) from Hitler's bunker. Hitler shot himself on April 30.

Key effects   The fall of Berlin brought World War II in Europe to an end.

Soviet troops close in on "Fortress Berlin" in April 1945.

FURTHER RESOURCES

PUBLICATIONS

Adams, Michael C.C., *The Best War Ever: America and World War II*, The Johns Hopkins University Press, Baltimore, Maryland, 1993.

Ambrose, Stephen E., *The Good Fight: How World War II Was Won*, Atheneum, New York, 2001.

Arthur, Max, *Forgotten Voices of World War II*, The Lyons Press, Guilford, CT, 2004.

Axelrod, Alan, *The Real History of World War II: A New Look at the Past,* Sterling, New York, 2008.

Brinkley, Douglas, *World War II Desk Reference,* Castle Books, New York, 2008.

Cross, Robin, *World War II*, DK Publishing, New York, 2007.

Darman, Peter, *Uniforms of World War II,* Bookmart, Leicester, UK, 1997.

Dear, I.C.B., and Foot, M.R.D., *Oxford Companion to World War II*, Oxford University Press, Oxford, UK, 2005.

Dickson, Keith D., *World War II for Dummies*, For Dummies, New York, 2001.

Dunnigan, James F., *Victory at Sea: World War II in the Pacific*, Harper Paperbacks, New York, 1996.

Gilbert, Martin, *The Holocaust: A History of the Jews of Europe During the Second World War,* Holt Paperbacks, New York, 1987.

Gilbert, Martin, *The Routledge Atlas of the Second World War*, Routledge, New York, 2008.

Gilbert, Martin, *The Second World War: A Complete History*, Holt Paperbacks, New York, 2004.

Grant, Reg, *World War II (DK Readers)*, DK CHILDREN, New York, 2008.

Hastings, Max, *Armageddon: The Battle for Germany, 1944–1945*, Vintage, London, 2005.

Hastings, Max, *Retribution: The Battle for Japan, 1944–45*, Knopf, New York, 2008.

Holmes, Richard, *World War II in Photographs*, Carlton Books, London, 2002.

Keegan, John, *Collins Atlas of World War II,* Collins, New York, 2006.

Keegan, John, *The Second World War,* Penguin, New York, 2005.

Overy, R.J., *The Origins of the Second World War,* Longman, Harlow, UK, 2008.

Purdue, A. W., *The Second World War*, Palgrave Macmillan, New York, 1999.

Shaw, Antony, *World War II: Day by Day,* Grange Books, Rochester, UK, 2000.

Shirer, William L., *The Rise And Fall Of The Third Reich*, Simon & Schuster, London, 1990.

Stokesbury, James L., *A Short History of World War II,* Harper Paperbacks, New York, 1980.

Stolley, Richard B., LIFE: *World War II: History's Greatest Conflict in Pictures,* Bulfinch, New York, 2005.

Tucker, Spencer, *The Second World War*, Palgrave Macmillan, New York, 2003.

Ward, Geoffrey C., and Burns, Ken, *The War: An Intimate History, 1941–1945*, Knopf, New York, 2007.

Weatherford, Doris, *American Women and World War II*, Castle Books, New York, 2008.

Weinberg, Gerhard L., *A World at Arms: A Global History of World War II*, Cambridge University Press, New York, 2005.

WEBSITES

www.worldwar-2.net
A complete World War 2 Timeline, detailing every event, day by day through World War II from 1939 through to 1945.

www.secondworldwar.co.uk
A general World War II resource, including important dates, casualty figures, high commands, and trivia.

www.ibiblio.org/pha
A collection of primary World War II source materials.

www.grolier.com/wwii/wwii_mainpage.html
The story of the war, biographies and articles, photographs, air combat films, and interactive test.

www.ess.uwe.ac.uk/genocide/WW2res.htm
Web Genocide Documentation Centre. World War II Resources.

www.war-experience.org
The Second World War Experience Centre.

INDEX